BUYING A
BETTER
WORLD

BUYING A
BETTER
WORLD

*George Soros
and Billionaire
Philanthropy*

ANNA PORTER

TAP
BOOKS

Editors: Diane Young and Bob Chodos
Design: BJ Weckerle
Indexer: Laurie Miller
Cover Design: Courtney Horner
Cover Image: Brendan Smialowski/Stringer, from Getty Images
Printer: Webcom

Library and Archives Canada Cataloguing in Publication

Porter, Anna, author
Buying a better world : George Soros and billionaire philanthropy / Anna Porter.

Issued in print and electronic formats.
ISBN 978-1-4597-3103-5 (pbk.).--ISBN 978-1-4597-3104-2 (pdf).--
ISBN 978-1-4597-3105-9 (epub)

1. Soros, George. 2. Open Society Foundations. 3. Philanthropists--
United States--Biography. 4. Capitalists and financiers--United States--
Biography. I. Title.

HV97.O6P67 2015   361.7'632092   C2014-907366-6
                                          C2014-907367-4

1   2   3   4   5   19   18   17   16   15

We acknowledge the support of the **Canada Council for the Arts** and the **Ontario Arts Council** for our
publishing program. We also acknowledge the financial support of the **Government of Canada** through the
Canada Book Fund and **Livres Canada Books**, and the **Government of Ontario** through the **Ontario Book
Publishing Tax Credit** and the **Ontario Media Development Corporation**.

Printed and bound in Canada.

TAP Books Ltd.
3 Church Street, Suite 500
Toronto, Ontario, Canada
M5E 1M2

VISIT US AT
www.dundurn.com/TAPbooks

To Julian,
who endured three years of my research,
travel, and writing

.

CONTENTS

SPREADING ACROSS THE WORLD

SOROS AND GLOBAL ISSUES

INTRODUCTION

George Soros is a legend. As a financial wizard who built a spectac-
ularly successful hedge fund, he rocked governments with highly
leveraged currency trades. As a philanthropist, he created a globally
active foundation whose mandate is based on his own often-contentious
ideas. He is a villain to his critics and a hero to those he has helped, who
are convinced that the world would be a worse place without him.

As befits a legend, a lot has been written about him. There have been
two biographies: Michael T. Kaufman's *Soros: The Life and Times of a
Messianic Billionaire* and Robert Slater's *Soros: The Life, Ideas, and Impact
of the World's Most Influential Investor*. Both authors go to great lengths
to point out that their books are not "authorized," although Kaufman
did have Soros's full cooperation, travelled with him, and attended some
meetings. Slater's book is a somewhat updated edition of his 1997 *Soros:
The Unauthorized Biography*. Slater wrote that Soros did not cooper-
ate with him the first time, but that he did for the new edition. Chuck
Sudetic's *The Philanthropy of George Soros: Building Open Societies* is
obviously a collaboration with his subject. Soros wrote a long essay for
the introduction, and Aryeh Neier, who was the president of Soros's
Open Society Foundations at the time, wrote the afterword. As a result,

it can hardly be expected to be an objective analysis of Soros's wide-ranging philanthropic enterprises.

Soros himself has written numerous books about his philosophy and his ideas for reforming the world. In recent years, he has been particularly busy writing about the financial crisis, the urgent need to save the European Union, and the almost equally urgent need to end the "war on drugs." In addition to his books, there are his articles, extensive interviews, his Open Society website, essays, lectures, and commentaries. There have been innumerable press releases from the various branches of his foundations. The anti-Soros right has not been idle either. They have been debunking Soros and what they believe he stands for in attack books, articles in a variety of right-wing journals, and blogs that picture him with horns and a tail as the "most evil man in America."

So, why another book?

Soros is eighty-four years old. This is his last active decade. He has been in feverish overdrive since his seventieth birthday, wishing to accomplish what he set out to do back in his fifties: inspire people to embrace "open society" and convince the world of intellectuals that his theories and ideas are fundamental to understanding the human condition. I have found it riveting to follow this messianic billionaire as he rushes to change the way we think. There is not much time left. I have focused on his current preoccupations and, looking back, measuring what he had set out to achieve and how it has worked out for him. Will his foundations survive him and, if so, in what form? Not long ago, he had assumed that they would not, that his philanthropic endeavors would end when he died. That assumption has changed.

As a philanthropist, he is unlike the Rockefellers, the Fords, or Bill and Melinda Gates in that he has been a social activist with very specific ideas about how to change the world. He has foundations in more than 100 countries, including Poland, Myanmar, Sierra Leone, Georgia, South Africa, Macedonia, Afghanistan, Liberia, Hungary, Estonia, and Haiti. Both the Bill and Melinda Gates Foundation and the Carnegie Foundation have narrower goals and are less likely to be steered away from their announced mandates than Soros's foundations. Open Society has been opportunistic in its approach to where it would focus.

Opportunism has been one of Soros's characteristics, both as an investor and as a philanthropist. He has been able to turn his attention to any new problem to try to solve it with new funds. His activities in Sarajevo are one example of fast action. His decision to become involved in Myanmar is another.

Soros is an idealist, a man who seems to believe that you can change the world to suit your benevolent theories, if only you spend enough money and are able to intervene at the right moment. He has spent about US $12 billion since 1985 in his efforts to change the way people think, and his foundations are continuing to spend his money at the rate of about $1 billion a year.

I decided to write about Soros and his foundations after criss-crossing central and eastern Europe to research my last book. I listened to people who had successfully influenced the course of history when their countries destroyed the Iron Curtain. The year was 2009, twenty years after Poland's famed round-table members had sat down to decide what kind of country they wanted. It was twenty years after Vaclav Havel, who had been jailed by the Communist government, was elected president of Czechoslovakia; twenty years after the ceremonial reburying of Hungary's 1956 revolutionary prime minister, Imre Nagy; and twenty years after the Berlin Wall was dismantled.

Wherever I went, I heard about George Soros. He had slipped money to Solidarity workers during the dark days of martial law in Poland, financed students' study tours to the West, supported dissidents and underground publications, purchased computer equipment for cash-strapped Russian universities, sold copying machines at ridiculously low prices to Hungarian libraries, and paid the substantial salaries of people like Harvard academic and Chicago School economist Jeffrey Sachs to help lay the plans for economic reforms. Some of those plans worked, others did not, but the point was that here was this American billionaire who was willing to put his own money into reforming moribund state-run economies.

No one kept track of how much Soros spent in those heady days of the pro-democracy forces. Soros himself had only a vague idea. Money was not a concern for him. Ideas were. As Morton Abramowitz of the

Carnegie Endowment for Peace once said, Soros is the only private citizen with his own foreign policy.

BY THE 1980s, Soros was already an inordinately wealthy man. As a speculator, he had created phenomenal earnings for his Quantum Fund, founded in 1969 with a borrowed $4 million that had grown to $100 million by 1980. It was the most successful hedge fund in the world, based offshore to avoid US taxes, trading in high-risk derivatives and options — a method that was then still in its infancy on capital markets. He often chose areas with scant regulation, such as currency trading. It was a high-risk business that required nerves of steel, and Soros was a master at it. He returned an average of more than 30 percent to investors, in contrast to the S&P 500 average of just over 10 percent during the same period of time. Then in 1992 he made a killing gambling against the pound.

Ten years earlier, Soros was telling interviewers that he did not believe in philanthropy. He had already created the Open Society Fund, but his motive was not primarily benevolent. The fund was set up as a charitable lead trust, which Soros described as "a very interesting tax gimmick" that allowed him to pass large sums to his heirs untaxed.[1] All that changed as he became more engaged with the causes he espoused. The foundation was no longer just a tax dodge. It had become an obsession.

He founded the Open Society Institute, later renamed the Open Society Foundations, in 1993, the year after he made a fortune short selling the pound. Its aims were nothing less than reforming societies and shaping public policy to reflect the values of liberal democracies. He believed that it was possible to change the way people think and, therefore, behave.

Those trying to understand his underlying investment theories flocked to his 1987 book *The Alchemy of Finance: Reading the Mind of the Market.* Anyone who picked it up with the expectation of learning how to become a billionaire, though, was sorely disappointed. Readers who wanted to understand how Soros's mind worked, on the other hand, might have found it rewarding. They would have learned something about his claim to have based his original ideas on those of renowned philosopher Karl Popper, whom Soros first encountered at the London School of Economics. Popper crops up in all of Soros's later books, along with theoretical physicist Werner Heisenberg and Soros's own theory of reflexivity. Though the term *open society* was first used by philosopher Henri Bergson, it was Popper who inspired Soros to give that name to his foundations. The reflexivity idea, although it has been described by other names, is his own. This theory has baffled heads of state and fellow public intellectuals since he first spoke about his basic adherence to its principles.

Being driven by a desire to see results is neither new nor unusual in the field of philanthropy. Being driven by a single idea is both. I wanted to explore how the Open Society behemoth spread its ideas of human rights, democracy, Western liberalism, and participatory capitalism. The Open Society Foundations brochure defines an open society as one "characterized by the rule of law; respect for human rights, minorities, and a diversity of opinions; democratically elected governments; market economies in which business and government are separate." How had those ideas translated into reality — or had they? In my pursuit of answers to that question, I spoke with Soros and most of his key lieutenants, along with former dissidents, students, politicians, journalists, economists, businessmen, academics, Soros's beneficiaries, and his detractors.

I HAD MET SOROS when he was in Toronto many years ago. Later, I talked to him when his friend Andy Sarlos, the Canadian arbitrage maven, was dying and wanted to see a positive quotation from Soros on the cover of his last book.[2] Andy was a friend of mine, and I was his publisher. Soros refused to shill for the book. He did not share Andy's views of the financial markets and, death or not, he was not about to compromise.

What took me to Soros's door again in 2012 were the activities of his Open Society Foundations and their various incarnations. I was interested in how they operate now, long after the central European catastrophe under Communism is over and its members have joined the European Union. So much has changed. Some of the early beneficiaries have become their countries' leaders, a few prime ministers and foreign ministers, renowned intellectuals, journalists, and successful businessmen. The great transformations are now part of history and, as the Western economies stumbled, Europe has again seen the rise of Fascism, racism, nationalism, and class hatred dragged back from the last century and parading down the streets and boulevards of Budapest, Vienna, Bucharest, Paris, Warsaw, Amsterdam, Rome, and Athens. Europe has faltered in its efforts to save the European Union. It has become divided along the lines of debtor and creditor nations. Soros's newest book, *The Tragedy of Europe,* sets out his theories about how to save the EU.

Soros's foundations have also been transformed. At the beginning of his philanthropic endeavors, Soros had not envisaged a large New York office. He wanted to support individuals who could deliver programs that he or his people thought were needed directly. During the last thirty-nine years, the New York office has grown to occupy an entire building and employ more than four hundred people.

The foundations' expenditures[3] are available for study on the Open Society Foundations' website. In 2013, the Justice Initiative spent almost $23 million, the Human Rights Initiative $51 million, the Initiative for Europe $19 million, the Criminal Justice Fund $17 million, the Campaign for Black Male Achievement Fund $6 million, and the Public Health Initiative $45 million. US programs, including the Institute for New Economic Thinking and Bard College, take up more than $120 million of Open Society's annual budget. Spending in Africa is close to $100 million and in Asia $43 million. In 2010, $12.3 million was expended on Burma alone, but by 2013 the Burma Project had shrunk to just over $8 million.

Soros himself has changed. During those twenty years, he has become a very public intellectual. He gives speeches and lectures, writes editorials, joins debates on the future of the European Union and capitalism, takes his concerns to heads of state, and dines with prime ministers, both past and present. Meanwhile, he has handed over the management of his philanthropic organizations to others. Hence the people around him — his key lieutenants in whatever country they inhabit — are more important than they had been earlier.

The foundations' presidency has recently passed from the human rights champion Aryeh Neier to the legalist Chris Stone. When Neier joined George Soros, both the aims and the structure of the organization adapted to Neier's own belief system. He was not selected accidentally. Before he went to work for Soros, Neier had launched Helsinki Watch, and later he founded Human Rights Watch. He had led investigations into human rights abuses throughout the world. He was instrumental in setting up the International Criminal Tribunal for the Former Yugoslavia. During his tenure, Open Society Foundations spent more than $2 billion to defend human rights. Viewed from this perspective, the past twenty-five years of Open Society have been the Neier years.

The future, under Stone's leadership, will be very different. When Soros announced Stone's appointment, he reiterated that he had been preoccupied with the future of his foundations and that the new president would have a "deep understanding of open society values, intellectual independence, and a commitment to justice." Stone has been reorganizing and restructuring the foundations, focusing more on justice and trying to reduce the role of the New York office.

IN 2010, MICROSOFT FOUNDER Bill Gates and billionaire investor Warren Buffett came up with the plan for the Giving Pledge: each man was to give away at least half of his fortune before he died. The Bill and Melinda Gates Foundation gave away about $25 billion, and Buffett pledged to donate 85 percent of his shares in Berkshire Hathaway, now increased to 99 percent of his total wealth. The two men then encouraged other rich people to join their enterprise. Dozens of them, including Britain's Richard Branson and Russia's Vladimir Potanin, flocked to the siren call of the two founders. Their plan was to avoid the standard charities and focus on outcomes.

Soros did not join them. At this late stage of his life, he still prefers to cut his own path. In addition to the Open Society Foundations, he established the Foundation to Promote Open Society in 2008. It had declared assets of $2.7 billion in 2012 and had distributed $257,940,437 in the same year. It seems to have the asset base to survive Soros. His Central European University in Budapest has been well endowed and established as a place for graduate students from all over the world. It is typical that Soros did not name the university after himself, just as he did not name his foundations after himself, unlike many of his fellow billionaires. He summed up his own sense of his charitable activities: "It gives me a sense of satisfaction to be engaged in an activity for which it would be worth dying."[4]

That statement is somewhat easier to make from the inside of a leased jet or from the palatial premises of Soros's residence and offices in New York than from ground level in Ukraine's Donetsk or from a Roma village in northeastern Hungary, but I have no doubt Soros meant it exactly as it sounded.

My quest with this book is to try to answer a question. In the end, what is likely to be his legacy?

THE MAN
AND
HIS IDEAS

ONE

The Messiah of Wall Street

George Soros, despite the wear and tear of more than eighty years, is a surprisingly fit and dapper presence. He has seemed in good shape on all occasions when I have seen him, including February 2014, after he had suffered a broken leg. The accident, he told me in somewhat self-deprecating tones, happened on the tennis court. He has a reputation for playing hard, competitive tennis. One of the young men recruited to fill in for a game in London said Soros was a formidable opponent, fast, powerful, and with a fine range of tricky shots at the net.

My first interview was in February 2012 in his vast, airy Seventh Avenue office. I crossed a shiny expanse of floor overlooked by huge windows and followed the stairs to where he had chosen to meet. The small boardroom's long table had nothing on it while the few volumes in the bookcase were his own. He was fashionably dressed in a sharply pressed grey suit that barely rippled as he approached. He wore an elegant blue and red tie, narrow and understated. His birdlike mien was reinforced by the very pronounced lines around his eyes, his large nose, and his thick, finely cut grey hair, swept upward like a tuft. He walked quickly, obviously in a hurry — the welcoming smile was fleeting and preoccupied — but he remained focused and polite throughout the time he spent with me, although I was aware of his frequent covert glances at Michael Vachon, his long-time political advisor and assistant. (The right-wing press calls Vachon his "consigliere."[1]) I found it interesting that Soros would care what his handler thought. He was a man who had chosen his own path in developing his philosophical framework of ideas, in building his enormous wealth, and dispensing much of it through his foundations.

At first he seemed surprisingly modest for a man who has admitted in another context that he has harboured "rather potent messianic fantasies ... since childhood" and had "an exaggerated view of my self-importance — to put it bluntly, I fancied myself as some kind of god."[2]

In its 2013 ranking of billionaires, *Forbes* estimated his net worth at $20 billion, which may explain why gorgeous young women like Brazilian bombshell Adriana Ferreyr and, more recently, Tamiko Bolton chose to spend so much time with him. Bolton, forty-two, and Soros, eighty-three, celebrated their marriage at his Bedford estate in September 2013. The reception, one of the most lavish evenings ever seen even in this elite part of the world, followed the next day. There was a hot air balloon made of flowers, the Budapest Festival Orchestra, heads of the World Bank and some eastern European countries, and five hundred of America's rich and famous. The dedication to Soros's newest book reads: "For Tamiko, without whom this book would not have been possible."

Meanwhile, Ferreyr, exhibiting the hallmarks of a spurned lover, sued for $50 million for emotional pain and her former lover's failure to buy her an apartment on East Eighty-Fifth Street. The case was dismissed, but the New York State appellate court did not immediately dismiss the assault charge the former actress brought against Soros.

One story told about Soros reveals that he had once been afraid of women. If so, he managed to conquer that fear fairly early. His marriage to Bolton is his third, and the last time I checked he was the father of five and had ten grandchildren.

SOROS WAS BORN Gyorgy Schwartz in 1930 in Budapest, Hungary. His middle-class Jewish family changed their name to Soros when the government began to pass increasingly restrictive and punitive anti-Semitic laws, leading up to joining Nazi Germany in its grand design to conquer Europe and, as part of that design, kill all Jews.

His father, Tivadar, was a bright, enterprising lawyer who had an odd enthusiasm for Esperanto (*soros* means "will soar" in that language). He had volunteered to serve in the Austro-Hungarian army for its First World War debacle, was captured by the Russians, and marched off to Siberia to labour in the mines. He escaped with a group of other Hungarian prisoners, survived the intense cold and the journey over mountains, made it through the 1917 Russian Revolution, and ended up in Moscow, where he founded an Esperanto association. In years to come, he credited his ingenious escape with teaching him the skills that his family needed to survive the Holocaust. Similarly, his son George, only fourteen years old in 1944 when the round-up of Hungarian Jews began, acknowledged his father's extraordinary ability to thrive in impossibly tough times.

Tivadar paid a government employee for false identity papers to help hide the family and instructed them on how to blend in with local gentiles. George became Sandor Kiss, a refugee from Romania. He accompanied his professed godfather on a tour of the Kornfeld estate — the home of a wealthy Jewish industrialist that the Nazis confiscated in exchange for allowing the Kornfelds to escape. In 2010, this episode returned to haunt Soros when Fox News' Glenn Beck accused him of having worked for the Nazis, stealing Jewish property while his fellow Jews were deported. Soros, usually at ease in responding to interview questions, was lost for words. The idea that he should feel guilty about surviving the Holocaust had never occurred to him, nor had he imagined that anyone could blame him for impersonating someone else in order to stay alive.

If the young George needed to see his father, it could be only at prearranged times, in front of one of public baths in the city. Soros proved to be so good at acting his part that he was able to beg cigarettes from Hungarian soldiers and turn them over to his father to trade.[3]

Even then, Soros thought of himself as someone apart, someone destined for greater things than those who obeyed orders to hand over their property and present themselves to the authorities. His father would not even consider the notion of obeying such orders. While most of the Jewish community did not believe the rumours about what would happen to them if they followed the government's orders, Tivadar Soros accurately predicted that doing what they were told would lead to being murdered. Despite seeing corpses in the street, young George was sure he would thwart the Nazis. "We were in mortal danger, but I was convinced I was exempt,"[4] he told one of his biographers.

In 1944, more than 400,000 Hungarian Jews were taken to Auschwitz-Birkenau in southern Poland. Most of them were killed on arrival in specially constructed gas chambers.

The Soros family survived.

Some tour guides now point out places where Soros and his family lived before 1944: a commodious apartment close to the wildly gothic parliament buildings and — in extended tours that include picturesque Szentendre — Lupa Island, where the Soros family spent summers. In his father's memoir, *Masquerade*, there is a photograph of young George, leaning on a hoe with a tilled field in the background. The picture was taken a year after the Germans left Hungary and the Russians moved in. George looks like a boy with a sunny disposition, cheerful, casually confident.

At seventeen, heeding Tivadar's advice, he left Soviet-ruled Hungary where, his father surmised, there would not be a suitable future for him. He went to London and eked out a meagre living, relying on charities while finishing his schooling. It was his confident attitude and a sense of entitlement that saw him through those first tough years in Britain and his unpleasant first encounter with philanthropy. Curiously, it was a Jewish charity's miserly response to the young Soros's request for money that may have coloured his views of Jewish charities for the rest of his life.

Soros graduated from the London School of Economics in 1952. Since then, he has become disillusioned with economics as a science, but he has retained an abiding admiration for philosopher Karl Popper, who was one of his professors. He has always credited Popper's work with providing the original philosophical framework for his own approach to making money and his own ideas about fairer, more open societies. "An open society," Popper said, "is not a perfect society but an imperfect society open to self-improvement." In open societies conflicting ideas could cheerfully coexist. Closed societies, dictatorships of all stripes, claim to possess the singular, ultimate truth and brook no opposition. Only brute force can ensure slavish adherence to the rules in such societies. Young Soros had already seen two dangerous dictatorships: Nazism and Stalinism.

Popper's book *Open Society and Its Enemies* was the inspiration for the name of Soros's foundations, and his political philosophy influenced not only Soros's own way of thinking, but his actions throughout his long life. It has provided him with a method of understanding truth and theory, distinguishing between reality and the individual's biased view of it. When dealing with the financial markets, Soros has been able to develop a method for anticipating events, such as booms and bubbles. As is the case in science, these predictions can be tested and verified. "The actual course of events then, serves as a test."[5]

Soros moved to the United States in 1956, the year his parents were finally able to leave Hungary, and found a job as a stockbroker. He started his hedge fund, later renamed the Quantum Fund, in 1969 with $4 million he raised from wealthy individuals who were convinced by his spiel about a new way to make a fortune. By 1980, the fund had grown to $100 million. By 1987, Quantum's assets were $21.5 billion. Over a thirty-year period, the fund returned an average of 31 percent to investors.[6] It became, in short order, the most successful hedge fund in the world, based offshore to avoid or delay US taxation. His was a game of trading derivatives and options, using maximum leverage. Observers praised his ability to stay detached and cool, no matter how high the bet; his willingness to admit he had made a mistake, cut his losses, and move on fast; and his capacity to act equally fast when he was sure he had made the right decision. Despite his occasional failures, he had enormous self-confidence. In 2013 alone, Quantum paid Soros $5.5 billion as it once again became the most successful hedge fund of all time.[7]

Today, he is one of the richest men in the world. *Fortune* ranked him thirtieth on its 2012 list of the wealthiest billionaires. (Mexico's Carlos Slim is number one and Bill Gates is number two.) He is the sixteenth wealthiest man in the United States, where he is both one of the most revered and one of the most attacked public figures. He is hated by those on the right for being too much of a leftie and by those on the left for being an unabashed capitalist. He commands front-page news throughout the world.

During our February 2014 interview in his Fifth Avenue apartment, a three-man German camera-crew was filming him for a national broadcast on his views about the future of the European Union. He is used to being trailed by cameras. He was less formally dressed than the last time I had seen him, but still elegant in an open-necked shirt, well-cut jacket, and slim grey pants. He looked a little more tired than a year earlier, but that's hardly surprising given his schedule of flying from one continent to another, attending meetings, getting married, and trying to persuade people that the European Union can still be a viable system despite the 2008 financial crisis and its aftermath.

Our interviews were wide-ranging and, although he sounded as if he had said most of it before, he did not guard his words. He talked about the World Economic Forum in Davos and his sense that, while everyone listened to him speak, it was hard to know to what extent he had influenced policy. Even if world leaders did not always act on his ideas, he felt they had had an effect.

He talked about the European Union and its problems. He discussed America's decline in influence, although it remains the dominant power in the world. He shared his thoughts about President Obama, Hungary, Poland, Wojciech Jaruzelski,[8] Vaclav Havel,[9] Vaclav Klaus,[10] and the prospects for Ukraine. He discussed the need for regulation in the financial markets and the difference between investing in financial markets and investing in principles. "In the one case," he said, "you do it to win. In the other, you do it to stand up for the principles — then sometimes a loss turns out to be a win."

His friend Leon Botstein, the president of Bard College and board chair of Central European University, told me that "George is an extremely cynical and pessimistic man. He has a darker, rather than lighter, view of human nature."[11] Bard has been a beneficiary of Soros's largesse, through his first wife's involvement in building the Bard Graduate Centre. He has been a member of several of Soros's boards. "Our role, as boards, has been more advisory than decision-making," he said, "but recently,

George has been pushing the boards to make more of the important decisions." Botstein is also the music director and principal conductor of the American Symphony Orchestra and teaches in the Department of History and Arts at Bard College. He said his friendships with both George Soros and Aryeh Neier may have been based on a shared background. His parents had also been survivors of the atrocities of war, had lost everything, and had to start over.

Soros's primary preoccupation since 2008 has been saving the European Union. He has already put forward several solutions to its problems, including Germany leaving the union so the others can devalue their currency (Angela Merkel was not interested); the creation of Eurobonds (Angela Merkel said "not while I am alive"); the forgiveness of a large portion of the debtor nations' debt; and so on.

"The EU was a fantastic idea when it was created by far-sighted statesmen, but now it's in the hands of a bunch of bureaucrats," he said in 2012. "Originally, they were dealing with reality and with how to improve it. Now they deal with sets of rules and how to bend them." He told *Newsweek* that if the euro collapses, if exclusions and small-mindedness win over sober reflection, "you have the danger of a revival of the political conflicts that have torn Europe apart over the centuries — an extreme form of nationalism ... xenophobia ... the exclusion of foreigners and ethnic groups." This process has already begun. In the build-up to the 2014 European Parliament elections, some of Europe's far-right parties have looked for common ground. Geert Wilders's Party for Freedom and Marine Le Pen's National Front have met to discuss shared opposition to Muslim immigration and to the European Union itself.

"Through self-inflicted mistakes the union has moved from solidarity to a relationship of debtors and creditors," Soros said.

By 2012, he had become pessimistic about the European Union's chances of survival. "Dissolution may become the line of least resistance. We are at the end of an era of relative stability in financial markets — with the Crash of 2008 as the banner year in the United States. Sadly, America's influence as a great power has declined. Naturally, this brings political instability, but if anyone thinks developments in Europe would not affect the rest of the world, they would be sadly mistaken."[12]

In 2012, he published a book of essays entitled *Financial Turmoil in Europe and the United States.* Essentially a critique of capitalism, it defines what Soros thinks about the financial mess the world has endured and will continue to endure unless major changes are made in regulating markets.

During our February 2014 interview, Soros was more optimistic. Angela Merkel, re-elected in 2013 as the Chancellor of Germany and the leader of Europe's strongest economy, hasn't listened to him so far, but he said that "Merkel's re-election makes it possible for her to reconsider. Now she has more discretion than she had before."[13]

While he abandoned his proposition that Germany leave the euro, he was still hoping for some form of Eurobonds. He was concerned about the prospect of deflation in Europe, favoured the French proposal for levying new corporate taxes that could be channelled to the neediest nations, and was seeking new ideas for saving the European Union. "Europe can't go on like this," he said.

His new book, *The Tragedy of the European Union: Disintegration or Revival,* goes back to offering solutions. Its publication was a couple of weeks away when we met for our interview, and that was why, Michael Vachon explained, my limited time with Soros had to be shared with the TV team from Germany. There was to be a *Spiegel Online* interview and extracts from the book, which he had co-authored with Gregor Peter Schmitz, former US correspondent for *Der Spiegel*, now Europe correspondent for *Spiegel Online.* Schmitz's interview with Soros also ran in *The New York Times Review of Books.*

Like most of the essays he writes for the *Financial Times* and *The New York Review of Books* and like most of his other books, the latest one is dense and abstruse, and it is equally unlikely to be taken to heart by the political elite in Europe or the United States. "Angela," as he told me, "is not likely to listen."

While waiting for the *Spiegel* crew to finish, I walked around Soros's splendid Upper East Side apartment, admiring the gold brocade couch, the green silk sofa with white silk cushions, the Japanese inlaid table, the Persian pink, blue, and ochre carpet, the Japanese cabinets, the antique mirror sideboard, and the abundance of books, some leather-bound, in the study overlooking Central Park.[14]

A few years ago, the *New Republic* called Soros "the single most powerful foreign influence in the whole of the former Soviet empire." Since then, his interests have broadened to include the battles for democracy in Myanmar, Liberia, Sierra Leone, Egypt, Zimbabwe, Haiti, Indonesia, Afghanistan, and Uzbekistan, among other places. His Open Society Foundations are among the most active charitable organizations in the world.

During the mid-nineties, he began taking a greater interest in what he saw as the erosion of democracy in the United States. He saw the Bush neoconservatives as a group of extremists who promoted the dangerous idea of American exceptionalism. In 2004 he invested $27 million in the losing campaign to keep George W. Bush out of the White House for a second term. If he was chastened by the experience of losing, he never admitted it. He told Bill Moyers in an interview that America Coming Together, the political action group he founded with fellow billionaire Peter Lewis, had met its goals in terms of voter turnout, and thus he had no regrets.[15]

Since 2008 he has contributed generously to Democratic political action committees (PACs), including direct funds to the Obama campaign,[16] but he has said he is disappointed in President Obama. "The problems confronting the United States are too big for any one man, but he could have provided better leadership. The comparison is as it was between Roosevelt and Hoover." Roosevelt had a vision, Hoover did not. But he said, disarmingly honest, there is another reason for his disappointment. "I couldn't establish a relationship with him."

As for how Obama felt about Soros, few were surprised to read in *FrontPage Mag* that, after listening to Soros's economic theories for forty-five minutes, Obama said, "I'm never f-ing sitting with that guy again." He qualified that by adding, "if we don't get anything out of him."

By 2014, Soros had pledged $250,000 to the committee supporting former US Secretary of State Hillary Clinton for president in 2016. His backing of Hillary is "an extension of his long-held belief in the power of grassroots organizing," explained Michael Vachon.[17]

In his book *The Crisis of Global Capitalism,* Soros predicted that the capitalist system was coming apart in the absence of a moral foundation and effective checks on its excesses. He contended that the deregulation of financial markets under the governments of Margaret Thatcher and Ronald Reagan and the ensuing "market fundamentalism" were responsible for the housing bubble, the Internet bubble, the super bubble, the crash of the late eighties, and the crisis that is still wreaking havoc in markets in the United States and Europe. The root of the problem, he said, is the misconception that the market, left to its own devices, will do the right thing. It won't.

"When I started my career in finance, banks and currencies were strictly regulated," he wrote in the *Financial Times,* although, most Soros-watchers know, as a fund manager he tried always to operate in areas of minimal regulatory oversight. Now it is time, he said, to return to regulations that can save the markets rather than destroy them. It was refreshing to hear him acknowledge, however, that few would listen to him on this point.

"I am a traitor to my class," he had admitted at the 2012 Davos World Economic Forum. "I think that income differentials are too great and ought to be narrowed." That would mean higher taxes for the rich, not a proposal the wealthy would gladly accept.

He talked of his hopes for the Institute for New Economic Thinking, which he had founded in 2009. The institute is now co-sponsored by Jim Balsillie, co-founder of Research in Motion (now BlackBerry), and William Janeway of Warburg Pincus. It has been a way of bringing together intellectuals to debate and discuss new ways of looking at economics and the financial problems besetting the world. He was enthusiastic about Lord Adair Turner, former chairman of Britain's Financial Authority, joining the group. He mentioned that Lord Turner had been working on a book of essays that could initiate new debate over the failures of the global financial system.

In addition to saving the European Union and proposing to reform the financial world, Soros's recent focus has included ending the US war on drugs. During our 2014 interview, he was exceptionally pleased with the support for abolition from South America and the two US states that have already abandoned strict drug laws.

"I don't want to have a memorial of my name after my death. I want to influence what's happening now," Soros said. Unlike others who have established foundations, Soros is willing — eager, according to Gara LaMarche, one of his former executives — to take big chances. With both financial markets and philanthropies, he is a gambler: "He doesn't believe in facilitators, consultants, advisors. He likes quick decisions."

"It's hard to find a fair criterion for judging success," Soros said. "This was brought home to me by Sergei Kovalev [a former Russian dissident, political prisoner, and biophysicist] who said, 'All my life I fought losing battles.'"

As hard as it is to see Soros as a failure, it is the view, he said, that he increasingly has of himself: "When I think of Russia today — the time and energy, the money I spent, seemingly to no avail ... " Some twenty years after he went to Moscow, full of hope and enthusiasm for encouraging reforms that never happened, we have seen the serial return of Vladimir Putin to power amid accusations of bribery, widespread election fraud, intimidation, and a complete disregard for democratic ideas. Soros was reluctant to admit any connection between what he had funded back in the glory days of his Russian idealism and today's protests in the streets of Moscow.

Still, the recent release from jail of his friend Mikhail Khodorkovsky, a Putin adversary, should have given him cause for hope. Shortly before our conversation took place in February 2014, they had had breakfast together. Given that meeting and all that was happening in the streets of Kyiv, Soros had something to celebrate. Vachon was quick to point out the breakfast was off the table for any news media.

In addition to being Soros's adviser on the Soros Fund, Vachon is a director of the Democracy Alliance, the Drug Policy Alliance, and the Institute for New Economic Thinking. He is also Soros's frequent spokesperson. He told me he briefed all Soros's senior executives on media relations, managed Soros's writing and public appearances, and acted as Soros's chief-of-staff for political contributions. In other words, he was one of the most powerful guys around Soros, the man you had to get through if you wanted to speak with Soros. He handled the press about Soros's Brazilian dalliance with Adriana Ferreyr. He is the guy who had to explain that Soros is not the chief funder of Occupy Wall Street and why the Soros Fund dumped its stake in gold. He seemed to carry borrowed power with the arrogance of someone who is accustomed to it and believes he deserves it.

Before our interviews, Vachon successfully convinced me that Soros has vastly more important matters to deal with than reviewing his legacy. Vachon implied that Soros has demands from his large family and personal issues to contend with and that he, Michael, was the best arbiter of what his daily focus should be. He referred to himself as "the gatekeeper to Soros's office" and made it clear on which side of the gate he thought I belonged.

It is not easy to manage a man like George Soros.

TWO

The Difficulty of Being Jewish

From the moment I said that I was going to write a book about George Soros's philanthropy, I have heard from a variety of Jewish friends who wanted to set me right about the damage Soros has done to Jewish causes. Some sent me links to websites that devote themselves to chronicling Soros's lack of sympathy or active denigration of Jewish endeavours, particularly those of Israel. Others sent articles about his charitable activities and how he has been critical of Jewish charities and unwilling to support Israel — the only democratic country in a sea of autocracies — even when it was attacked by Palestinians.

Being Jewish is complicated. It is particularly complicated in post-war North America where Jewishness is often defined in ways that would baffle even Jews themselves. For funny and thoughtful explorations of this subject, read Mordecai Richler's *Joshua Then and Now* or almost any one of his other novels.

For Soros, a man constantly in the public eye, it has proven particularly difficult to define his relationship to his Jewishness. Like Mordecai Richler, he has been accused both of anti-Semitism and of Jewish elitism. Like Jews under the Nazis and in much of the Arab world, he has been accused of far-left Marxist activities as well as of extreme capitalism (i.e., accumulating wealth in order to rule the world). Some have succeeded in levelling both charges simultaneously, a feat that defies logic, except for those who are still reading *Protocols of the Elders of Zion*, the 1903 anti-Semitic hoax. To prove its ability to appeal to the deeply uneducated and hate-filled, Egyptian television produced a successful forty-one-part mini-series based on the *Protocols*.

While he readily acknowledges his Jewishness, Soros has never presented himself as a Jew, sought out Jewish audiences, or chosen Jewish charities for his philanthropic endeavours. The last time he did seek out a Jewish charity, it was to ask for support while he was studying in London shortly after his arrival from Hungary, and it was not a satisfying occasion.

He has said that his Jewishness did "not express itself in a sense of tribal loyalty." Rather, he defined himself as "an outsider," willing to see other points of view. He has been generally indifferent to his Jewishness. He is neither a believer nor a joiner, nor does he have any Jewish community ties.

One of the most complicated aspects of being Jewish has to do with how one relates to Israel. Strong support for Israel has been a hallmark of North American Jewry, and especially of its most powerful voices such as the American Israel Public Affairs Committee, the influential pro-Israel lobby in the United States. These voices often treat any criticism of Israel as tantamount to treason. At the same time, many North American Jews are critical of specific Israeli policies and actions, such as West Bank settlements or the blockade of Gaza, while remaining supportive of Israel's existence. Soros's support for these elements in the community and his own statements critical of the policies of Israel and its American backers have added fuel to the fire of his detractors. "I don't deny Jews the right to a national existence," he told *New Yorker* writer Connie Brook, "but I don't want to be part of it."

At a gala dinner in Budapest on May 13, 2003, sponsored by YIVO, the New York-based institute for the study of Jewish culture, Soros talked of some victims becoming victimizers. His role that evening should have been to present an award to another Holocaust survivor, author Imre Kertesz, winner of the 2002 Nobel Prize for literature, but, much to the chagrin of the audience, he decided to talk about current Israeli-Arab politics as well.

In November 2003, when he spoke to the Jewish Funders Network in New York, he talked about his support for projects in Palestine and placed part of the blame for the rise of anti-Semitism in Europe at the time on the policies of the State of Israel. Much to the shock and astonishment of his audience, he said, "There is a resurgence of anti-Semitism in Europe. The policies of the Bush administration and the Sharon administration contribute to that … If we change that direction, anti-Semitism will diminish."

That same year, he also seemed to lend credence to Malaysian Prime Minister Mahathir Mohamed's charge that "Jews rule the world by proxy." After all, his own funding of governments and political causes had influenced world affairs, and he was clearly a Jew. Jewish influence was "an unintended consequence" of his own actions, he said, and had contributed to anti-Semitism.

The sound of pro-Israel outrage was even noisier than the fury Soros usually elicited from the conservative right. Jewish writers and commentators charged him with defending anti-Semitism and providing a platform for accusations of the "international Jew" who could control the world. None of the accusations appeared to deter Soros from continuing to express his opinions. He would remain an internationalist, not part of any tribe.

In a 2007 article in *The New York Review of Books*, he tried to explain his position: "I do not subscribe to the myths propagated by enemies of Israel and I am not blaming Jews for anti-Semitism. Anti-Semitism predates the birth of Israel … at the same time, I do believe that attitudes toward Israel are influenced by Israel's policies, and attitudes toward the Jewish community are influenced by the pro-Israel lobby's success in suppressing divergent views."

In 2007 in an article for the *Financial Times*, he argued that Israel and the United States should accept the challenges of dealing with Hamas because it had won a democratic election. Designating it a terrorist organization did not promise peace for either Israel or the Palestinians.

Leon Botstein, who describes himself as a Zionist, an active member of the Jewish community, and a lifelong supporter of Israel, was quick to point out to me that on this issue, as in all matters, Soros welcomes a debate. The two of them have often chewed over these questions, but at no time has Botstein's stance on Israel been a barrier to his many appointments to Soros's boards. "The only people he dislikes," Botstein said, "are sycophants."

"Some US supporters of Israel are more rigid and ideological than the Israelis themselves," Soros wrote in February 2011, accusing Israel of not being able to recognize its own best interests. He made this statement in an article supporting the revolution in Egypt and the Muslim Brotherhood, an organization not known for embracing diversity or an open society.

A year earlier, Fox News host Glenn Beck had hosted a two-part program on Soros. During the course of the program, Beck stated that Soros "used to go around with this anti-Semite and deliver papers to the Jews and confiscate their property and then ship them off … Here's a Jewish boy helping send the Jews to the death camps." Beck also accused Soros of operating a shadow government with the avowed aim of destroying the US system.

Beck's tirade was an old-fashioned, garden-variety anti-Semitic attack, alleging a wide-ranging Jewish conspiracy that aimed to take over the world. Such attacks have always found fertile ground in some quarters, mostly among members of the uneducated underclass in Europe. With barely a pause, Beck then managed the double-whammy of accusing Soros himself of anti-Semitism. He dredged up the bit about Soros hiding from deportation to Auschwitz by impersonating a Christian boy while his fellow Jews were transported and used it against him.

Fortunately, many people came to Soros's defense, including leaders of the Jewish establishment. J.J. Goldberg, the former editor-in-chief of *The Forward*, America's leading Jewish newspaper, described Beck's attack as being "as close as I have heard on mainstream television to fascism." The Anti-Defamation League, not normally a Soros ally, condemned Beck. Its national director, Abraham Foxman, came out with: "Glenn Beck's description of George Soros' actions during the Holocaust is completely inappropriate, offensive and over the top … to hold a young boy responsible for what was going on around him during the Holocaust as part of a larger effort to denigrate the man is repugnant."

While that statement is true, it is still difficult to comprehend Soros's description of the Holocaust years in Hungary as "the most exciting time of my life."[1] Or his more recent remark that Israel is the main stumbling block to American attempts to foster Egypt's demand for democracy.

Considering that Soros has given more than $12 billion to various causes worldwide, many Jewish groups believe that the funding he gives to Jewish charities is insultingly small. Yet he does donate. In 2010 he gave $1 million to ORT, a Jewish educational foundation with offices around the world, to develop a program to help Liberia's former child soldiers,[2] and in 2012 the Soros Fund Charitable Foundation contributed $825,000 to fifteen synagogues and schools.

A donation that Soros made in 2010 to J Street, an organization that defines itself as "The Political Home for Pro-Israel, Pro-Peace Americans," might sound like an example of support for a pro-Israel organization. A closer examination of J Street's origins and objectives, however, presents a somewhat different picture. J Street was set up in 2008 as a liberal alternative to the American Israel Public Affairs Committee. AIPAC identifies itself as the "Pro-Israel Lobby," while J Street leaders have demanded that Israel lift the closure of Gaza and initially opposed harsher sanctions against Iran.[3] Such statements have been enough for right-wing backers of Israel to put J Street on their enemies list. According to the J Street website, Soros and his family have since since provided yearly contributions of $500,000, representing about 7 percent of J Street's budget.[4]

Apart from J Street, Soros funds, to a greater or lesser degree, several other non-profit groups that are critical of Israel. Media Matters and Center for American Progress are two examples that have been noted.[5]

In addition, Soros's Open Society Foundations are a major supporter of Human Rights Watch, an NGO that has been repeatedly criticized for its disproportionate condemnation of Israeli interventions in the Palestinian Territories. It joined other international NGOs in its condemnation of Israel's military intervention in Jenin, the "massacre" that never happened, based on a report that was withdrawn by its author. Known for its careful documentation of human rights abuses, Human Rights Watch's annual reports have frequently emphasized Israel's actions, while ignoring horrendous human rights abuses in Arab countries. When Human Rights Watch's founder, publisher Robert Bernstein, attacked it for its uneven treatment of Israel, the only "open society" in the Middle East, Aryeh Neier, his former colleague and now president of Open Society, accused Bernstein of ignorance of the issues facing open and closed societies. He denied that Human Rights Watch was biased against Israel.

In his November 2006 response to the "Attack on Human Rights Watch,"[6] Neier defended the organization's report of the killing of twenty-one civilians, including children, fleeing the Lebanese border village of Marwahin. Aerial attacks from Israeli helicopters were responsible for these deaths, and Human Rights Watch was perfectly correct in recording what had happened.

Among other organizations that Soros has supported is the Institute for Middle East Understanding, whose website features a range of pro-Palestinian and anti-Israel reports. Its president, Jaleh Bisharat, accused Israel of war crimes and its secretary stated that Israel was an "apartheid" state.[7] Soros's Open Society Foundations have also been a frequent supporter of Amnesty International, another human rights group that has been accused of focusing disproportionately on Israel, accusing it of being "an apartheid state," and writing about "the collective punishment" of Palestinians. Amnesty International has also supported an arms embargo against Israel and lawsuits against it in the International Criminal Court.[8]

In 2011, in an article for *The Washington Post*, Soros extolled the virtues of the Arab Spring revolutions, in particular the ones in Tunisia and Egypt. He claimed that "the main stumbling block" to dignity in Egypt is Israel, whose "US supporters are more rigid and ideological than the Israelis themselves." He added that as a proponent of democracy and open society, he shared in the enthusiasm sweeping across the Middle East. "In reality, Israel has as much to gain from the spread of democracy in the Middle East as the United States has. But Israel is unlikely to recognize its own best interests because the change is too sudden and carries too many risks," he wrote in his February 2011 *Washington Post* editorial.

That year he was also accused of being an active supporter of the Muslim Brotherhood[9] and of Mohamed ElBaradei for president of Egypt. ElBaradei, an Egyptian law scholar, former diplomat, and director general of the International Atomic Energy Agency, had been a member of the International Crisis Group's board of trustees and briefly the vice president of Egypt. He is now in exile.

Open Society has also supported some local NGOs, including Al-Haq which was listed as a terrorist organization by the US State Department; Al-Mezan in Gaza and B'Tselem in Israel, both outspoken critics of Israel's human rights record; and Adalah, the Legal Centre for Arab Rights in Israel.

In 2013 NGO Monitor, a pro-Israel self-described "research organization," published a monograph by Alexander Joffe and Gerald Steinberg entitled *Bad Investment: Philanthropy of George Soros and the Arab-Israeli Conflict. How Soros-Funded Groups Increase the Tensions in a Troubled Region.* The publication includes a plethora of innuendo and accusations: the Open Society Institute based in Zug, Switzerland, is called "rather secretive" and Soros and his family support organizations are described as waging "an intensive campaign of delegitimization and political warfare targeting Israel."

In *Soros on Soros: Staying Ahead of the Curve*, he writes, "I am proud of being a Jew — although I must admit it took me practically a lifetime to get there. I have suffered from the low self-esteem that is the bane of the assimilationist Jew. This is a heavy load that I could shed only when I recognized my success."[10]

Despite his denials, then, it appears as if Soros has always felt himself to be "one of the tribe." Like many other Holocaust survivors I have known, however, he refuses to be viewed as anyone's victim … except, perhaps, his own.

I watched George Soros on June 27, 2014, in a commemoration of the so-called "Star Houses" in Budapest — houses marked with a star when Hungary was a Fascist ally of Germany during the Second World War. By then, Jews had already been forced to wear the yellow star, although the Soros family was not among them because Soros's father had anticipated the move and obtained false identity papers. The day was organized by the Open Society Foundation's Archives. He seemed to be very moved by the occasion as he sat on an uncomfortable backless stool in front of a building where he had hidden briefly as a boy, during the time when it was fatal to be Jewish in Hungary.

THREE

The Ideas That Fuel the Man and His Foundations

"Ever since I became conscious of my existence, I have had a passionate interest in understanding it," George Soros said in *The Alchemy of Finance*. When this book was published in 1987, he was already celebrated in US financial circles, but he had not yet become "The Man Who Broke the Bank of England." His Quantum Fund was one of the first hedge funds to use derivatives, taking extraordinary risks, leveraging each move beyond what the fund could access from its own banks. Short selling is a game that requires nerves of steel and sharp instincts for where the market is heading, not only day by day, but minute by minute. Soros has these in spades.

When Soros named his fund Quantum in 1979, it was in honour of German theoretical physicist, Werner Heisenberg, whose "uncertainty principle" in quantum theory had been one of the chief influences in Soros's own thinking. The theory, discounting its more complex facets that led to Heisenberg's Nobel Prize for physics, meshes nicely with Soros's own theory of reflexivity. During our last meeting, Soros again referred to Heisenberg and quantum physics as a great way to understand his own philosophy. He seemed delighted with its continued relevance.

In Heisenberg's theory, the act of measuring one property in a system introduces irreducible uncertainty into other properties in the system. As a result, there is a degree of inaccuracy in any attempt to measure all the system's properties. In Soros's theory, the act of studying something affects one's observation of the subject studied, which then changes the subject itself, and so on, in a reflexive arc. In *Soros on Soros* he wrote that this view of the world means that our generally accepted notion of truth needs to be re-examined. "We need to recognize that there are more than just the two categories: true-false." The third category is "reflexive."

Soros concluded while he was still a student of Karl Popper's that economics was not a science, despite its efforts to model itself along Newtonian physics. It is not and cannot be objective. It is impossible to test its tenets without affecting its predictions. People themselves, as thinking participants, influence economic life; therefore, they could not describe it from the outside. Moreover, as participants, they influence outcomes.

Frequently, he has referred to his youthful enthusiasm for Popper as the beginnings of his own critical thinking. In Popper's thought, an open society is one that allows a full range of ideas and convictions to peacefully coexist because there is recognition that no one possesses the ultimate truth. Unlike dictatorships, whether of the left or the right, the government does not try to dictate human behavior.

Popper championed liberal democracy against authoritarianism and totalitarianism. He also held that human knowledge is "irreducibly hypothetical"; that is, it cannot be proven, although it can be "falsified." We can conjecture from past experience, but we cannot be absolutely sure. According to Popper, truth is beyond human authority. In his book *Conjectures and Refutations: The Growth of Scientific Knowledge*, he proposed that all scientific theory is conjecture and inherently fallible.

Popper suggested that we "give up the idea of ultimate sources of knowledge, and admit that all knowledge is human; that it is mixed with our errors, our prejudices, our dreams, and our hopes; that all we can do is to grope for truth even though it be beyond our reach. We may admit that our groping is often inspired, but we must be on our guard against the belief, however deeply felt, that our inspiration carries any authority, divine or otherwise."[1]

These ideas are echoed in Soros's own philosophy. He believes that our view of the world is affected by our personal history, our education, and the timing of our observations, and thus it has no correspondence to a scientifically ascertainable truth. Furthermore, every person's perception of the universe is different from every other person's. Therefore, we all live with uncertainty in all our observations.

Soros believes that he has been able to improve on his original ideas in successive years, because he has been able use his theories to model the "boom-bust" process of financial markets.

What readers found in *The Alchemy of Finance*, first published in 1988, was Soros's effort to describe how the world works, and his desire to share his thoughts with those who could follow in his intellectual steps. It is not easy.

Soros explained his financial success by referring to his philosophy. "The only competitive edge I have is the theory of reflexivity," he said.[2] "What one thinks is part of what one thinks about, therefore, one's thinking lacks an independent point of reference by which it can be judged — it lacks objectivity."[3] This leads to the conclusion that all our views of the world are flawed. Moreover, we influence what we observe by our observation, thus ending with a neat circle of seeing-understanding-changing-seeing-understanding, and so on. "On the one hand, the participant seeks to understand the situation in which he participates ... On the other hand, he seeks to make an impact. When both functions are at work at the same time I call the situation reflexive."[4]

Later, Soros tried to explain the theory again: "The major insight I bring to understanding things in general is the role that imperfect understanding plays in shaping events."[5]

And still later, he tried once more: "I can state the core idea in two relatively simple propositions. One is that in situations that have thinking participants, the participants' view of the world is always partial and distorted. That is the principle of fallibility. The other is that these distorted views can influence the situation to which they relate because false views lead to inappropriate actions. That is the principle of reflexivity ...Traditional economics is based on theories of equilibrium, where supply and demand are equal. But if you realize what an important role our imperfect understanding plays, you realize that what you are dealing with is disequilibrium."[6]

Soros claimed that this revelation, when it was applied to the market, formed the basis of his financial wizardry. "Market participants operate with a bias and that bias influences events."[7] In Soros's view, "economic man," who makes rational decisions, is merely a construct of economists. He does not exist. Although economists recognize this idea, they have had great difficulty working it into their theories.

Susan Porter of Forex Crunch agreed that Soros's theory of reflexivity is a useful tool for evaluating the reactions of the market. She made a brave effort to narrow down its applicability by observing, "It essentially refers to a circular relationship moving between cause and effect, with both affecting each other in a self-referencing economic symbiosis."[8]

In 2012 when Soros described the events leading up to the 2008 "crash," he blamed "market fundamentalism," the belief that, left to their own devices, markets will self-correct.[9] They do not. Markets are driven by investors' views of reality, which means prices tend to overshoot on the way up in an up-market and on the way down in a down-market. Investors, inadvertently, justify their own expectations. Their own biases cause a stock to rise or fall.

"The crux of reflexivity is not so obvious; it asserts that market prices can influence the fundamentals. The illusion that markets manage to be always right is caused by their ability to affect the fundamentals they are supposed to reflect."[10]

Soros's theory of reflexivity can be found in all of his books. Sometimes it takes up the whole book; at other times it is just there in large, undigested chunks. It spreads into his essays, his speeches, his pronouncements, lectures, and discourses. In the preface to his most recent book to date, *The Tragedy of the European Union: Disintegration or Revival*, renowned economist Anatole Kaletsky tries valiantly to give reflexivity another shove: "This interference between perceptions and realities creates waves of instability in markets and political systems."

Soros is not alone in giving economists a failing grade for missing the signs that led to the crash of 2008 and for their blindness to the limitations of human rationality, but he is the only market participant to have made a life philosophy out of observing the limitations of economics.

For him, reflexivity is a philosophy of the world, of all major events in human lives. The market merely provided an easy testing ground for the grand ideas. Those who are active in the market make constant value judgements, which will, of course, affect what they are valuing. Soros claimed this had been the guiding principle of his success. In other words, he was able either to discount the loop of the market or see it in advance of others.

Soros's 1995 lecture at Vienna Institute of Human Sciences was titled "A Failed Philosopher Tries Again." Once again, he tried to explain the philosophy behind his lifetime of financial success and his philanthropic enterprise. He started simply enough with, "My philosophy can be summed up in one phrase: a belief in our own fallibility ... The misconceptions and misunderstandings that go into our decisions help shape the events in which we participate." But then, he fell off the horse, "Fallibility plays the same role in human affairs as mutation does in biology."

In 2012 he gave it another try: "On the one hand, people seek to understand the situation ... on the other, they seek to make an impact on the situation ... the two functions form a circular relationship or feedback loop." He talked again about fallibility or "imperfect understanding" and its effects on people's decisions.

Soros, the billionaire speculator, has sought to be respected for his philosophy and his ideas, not for his financial acumen. What his success has afforded him, he said, is a platform; the right to be listened to, even when people lack the necessary tools to understand him.

Professor Janos Kis, a former Hungarian dissident and now a distinguished philosopher on Central European University's faculty, says the solution to Soros's problem of not being taken seriously as a philosopher is to abandon that particular ambition. He is unable to express his ideas in terms to which academic philosophers pay attention or students and the general public can read and understand. "His intuitions are truly interesting, but the way he expresses them prevents them from being taken seriously," he told me.

He suggested a change in Soros's ambition. Soros should reshape himself as a "public intellectual," with ideas in different domains. As a public intellectual he would receive more recognition. He would be judged by the trajectory of other such intellectuals, people like Michael Ignatieff, Francis Fukuyama, Ivan Krastev, André Glucksmann, and Timothy Garton Ash — a stellar cast in whose ranks he would easily fit. It's good advice, and Soros seems to have followed it. He is viewed by many as a public intellectual. But would he be offered an audience if he wasn't also one of the richest men on earth?

There is strange contradiction in Soros's blaming "market fundamentalists" and the governments that have allowed them free rein. He said he believed that globalization and new, complex, hard-to-analyze financial instruments have made markets overly volatile and that government intervention is therefore not only appropriate, but necessary. He explained that newfangled financial instruments — such as collateralized debt obligations and credit default swaps — have been beyond the ability of regulators to regulate. They simply do not understand them.

Yet Soros, the speculator, made his fortune in unregulated markets, managing to evade taxes, and as his fame and fortune grew, even moving markets in one direction or another. Using his theory of reflexivity, he has damaged some national economies. The fact that he devotes a large share of his profits to charity does not lessen his responsibility for "moving markets."

When he stated in 2000 that he had succeeded in integrating "the various aspects of my existence,"[11] one has to wonder how he managed it. To examine whether he has really succeeded, one needs only to look at the effect of his 1998 warning letter to the *Financial Times*, recommending a modest devaluation of the ruble. It caused financial markets to flee the Russian currency, Russian debts defaulted, and the Russian prime minister resigned. The crisis that he was so keen for Russia to avoid became a reality, in part because of his meddling. On the other hand, this instance could have been a perfect example of reflexivity — or the paradox of unintended consequences.

It is easy to agree with Soros's current view that capitalism no longer works even for those for whose benefit it was invented, let alone for the millions who have been left with little hope of recovering their losses after the most recent economic crash. But he has not proposed a viable alternative.

The question remains whether some alterations in the global financial system would alleviate the pain for the majority watching from the sidelines as the fabulously wealthy 1 percent make a killing. Soros is, of course, a member of that 1 percent.

In *Soros on Soros*, he contemplates his place in history and suggests that he has had a real impact in the countries where his foundations operate. But, he ponders, "Can I make a mark with my ideas? Can I communicate them? Are they valid? That is what matters to me most." As for the concept of open societies, he sees it more as a policy goal. In a world of disorder, the old spirits of nationalism can easily triumph over rationalism, and dictatorships can replace fragile democracies. To cap it all, Soros adds as an appendix to the book an essay on his favorite theme — reflexivity.

For his seventieth birthday in 2000, a group of distinguished friends and admirers produced a book of essays to honour him. The title was *The Paradoxes of Unintended Consequences*. It is an interesting way to examine Soros's philanthropic endeavours, and it suits Soros's philosophy well. He believes that almost all human efforts suffer from unpredictable results. Even the very act of examining a sequence of current events can, and usually does, change its course and its end result. The observer becomes an unintended participant in what he is observing.

Soros, at more than eighty-four years of age, rich beyond avarice, is not about to give up on his ideas. He travels to universities and conferences to talk about what he considers to be the important issues of the day and about how reflexivity works. In 2009 he delivered a series of five lectures at Budapest's Central European University. "I hope that my ideas will be received in the same spirit of critical thinking in which they are offered and not as some sort of dogma," he said in his introduction.

It is interesting to watch the lectures on video. Soros seems to be thoroughly enjoying himself. He is willing to have his ideas debated, discussed, disagreed with, and even denigrated, if that's what it takes to bring them to an engaged public.

The Tragedy of the European Union, a book in interview form that is rather repetitive and not Soros's best, includes a massive Appendix: "Fallibility, Reflexivity, and the Human Uncertainty Principle." It is one more extensive stab at explaining his ideas. This time he has added a few illustrations and thrown in a "Conceptual Framework" and the "Boom-Bust Process." It ends with the announcement that the *Journal of Economic Methodology* is publishing a special issue on reflexivity. Soros is delighted with that prospect. He hopes it will provide a forum to discuss, debate, and even debunk his ideas, but at least they will be taken seriously.

"He is a global statesman," said Gara LaMarche, stating the obvious. "He can pick up the phone and call anyone anywhere" and expect his call will be answered. But it is not enough. "George would like to be remembered for his ideas." These are at the heart of his world view and philanthropy. It is disheartening for him to know that the ideas he has put forward in his books and myriad articles have not been taken seriously. Upon receiving an honorary degree at Oxford University he said, "I would like to be called a financial, philanthropic and philosophical speculator."[12]

His friend Joseph Stiglitz, the Nobel Prize–winning economist, said in an online interview that one of the refreshing characteristics of Soros's approach to ideas is that he is willing to listen, learn, and debate — and do so in a public forum.

THE OPEN
SOCIETY
FOUNDATIONS

FOUR

Mr. Human Rights

There can be no serious discussion of the achievements of George Soros's Open Society Foundations or of his legacy without considering Aryeh Neier's leadership of the foundations, which lasted almost twenty years. Neier was the formative force that steered the foundations' course and, while he paid attention to Soros, it is also true that Soros paid a great deal of attention to him.

It was in the offices of Helsinki Watch that Soros began to formulate his own approach to philanthropy, and it was the prospect of Neier's retirement that propelled him to think, once again, about the mission and the future of his foundations.

A well-worn saying about Neier has it that if Soros is the only American citizen with a foreign policy all his own, then Neier is his secretary of state. He is tall, slightly stoop-shouldered, thin, with very expressive hands, even when his face is set in the somewhat forced, patient smile that he wears when he listens. He is a quiet, somewhat doleful presence. He speaks slowly, with almost equal emphasis on every phrase, irrespective of the highs and lows of his message. In the hours I spent with him, I saw him flare up only once: when I asked him about his former colleague Bob Bernstein's attack on Human Rights Watch, the organization Neier had led to prominence and one of Open Society's most consistent funding recipients. In an opinion piece for *The New York Times*, Bernstein noted that recently, "Human Rights Watch has written far more condemnations of Israel for violations of international law than of any other country in the region."[1]

"How could Bob condemn HR's activities without supporting data? And how could he charge that it is anti-Israel?" Neier observed that it is not Human Rights Watch's task to sort out who started the attacks. The organization simply observes events and applies an equal measure of judgement to both sides of the conflict.

Impeccably polite, he stood when I entered his office and waited until I was settled on his low sofa before he sat on his higher, straight-backed chair. I have met him several times, but each time he gave the impression that I needed to introduce myself.

Neier was born in Berlin in 1937 into a middle-class Jewish family. His parents, fearing the probability of a Nazi state more than the uncertainty of immigration, left for Britain in August 1939, two weeks before the invasion of Poland and just three months before Kristallnacht — the night of broken glass that put to rest all hopes for Jewish survival in Nazi Germany.

He has scant memories of his first few months in Britain, but what he recalls is profound misery in a hostel for refugee children, separated from his parents, unable to understand the language, and being frequently confined to a corner of the playroom. In his autobiography, *Taking Liberties: Four Decades in the Struggle for Rights*, Neier says, "I attribute my lifelong preoccupation with prisons and other institutions used for confinement to my loathing for that hostel." It is not too difficult to connect his childhood experiences with his battles to defeat injustice, although it is more difficult to understand why he thought it necessary in 1978 to have the American Civil Liberties Union support the National Socialist Party of America, a self-professed neo-Nazi group, in its decision to march through the Chicago-area town of Skokie, where a large number of Holocaust survivors had settled. The ACLU, intractably attached to the freedom of speech principle, fought in court for the group's right to march wearing Nazi uniforms and insignia, no matter how offensive this was to the residents. In some ways, this battle was typical of the young Neier's purist views.

The ACLU lost about 30,000 members as a result. Neier was the executive director at the time and while those losses might have worried another kind of leader, it made no difference to Neier. He was always sure of the rightness of his decisions.

He was only twenty-five when he joined the ACLU, then engaged in battles defending draft opponents and the right of Americans to protest the war in Vietnam.

The day the board adopted a resolution calling for the impeachment of President Richard Nixon — September 30, 1973 — was one of his proudest memories of his time at ACLU. The Watergate scandal had already dominated the nation's newspapers for several months, and federal departments had all but ceased to function while everyone watched as the disaster unfolded. It was the first time in US history that a sitting president was publicly accused of authorizing burglary, electronic surveillance, and the use of the Internal Revenue Service and other government agencies to spy on US citizens. While the ACLU's action may have been symbolic, "it was the first national organization to take a stand," Neier wrote in *Taking Liberties.*

Each chapter covering Neier's ACLU years details a different action, but all are focused on guaranteeing personal freedoms. Most actions continued as favoured causes during his ensuing years heading other organizations and speaking on behalf of other groups he was determined to defend. His causes included confronting police abuse, defending draft opponents, legalizing abortion, and forging restraints on stigma.

"Neier is a believer in absolute moral codes, an ideologue," noted political scientist and fellow Open Society stalwart, Ivan Krastev.

In 1978, Neier launched Helsinki Watch with Random House's president, Bob Bernstein, and prominent lawyer Orville Schell, Jr. Initially, its purpose was to protest the persecution of Soviet citizens who were drawing the West's attention to the Soviet Union's infractions of the Helsinki Treaty on Human Rights, a treaty signed by the Soviet leaders. It provided the first wedge into a monolithic Soviet system of repression, and it was the first time, as far as the outside world knew, that

Russians had dared to openly protest. Neier thought the partnership was ideal: Bernstein provided the public passion and Schell the blessings of a legal luminary while he served the cause behind the scenes. His own strengths included tenacity and the hard work to back it up. His passion for justice was equal to Bernstein's, but he preferred to avoid emotional displays. "My style," he said with his usual understatement, "was reserved."

He was encouraged when the Nobel Prize was awarded to Amnesty International, the first time human rights had been recognized by the Stockholm judges.

The CIA's role (under Nixon and Kissinger) in bringing about the 1974 Pinochet coup in Chile and the subsequent murders and torture of the military regime's opponents was the inspiration for the founding of Americas Watch, a committee set up by the same trio who had set up Helsinki Watch. Under Neier, it took issue with the Reagan administration's policies in other South American countries where the CIA played a lead role. Americas Watch attacked the Reagan administration's policies in El Salvador, Guatemala, Argentina, and, of course, Chile. As the founders were also engaged in protesting Soviet repression, they could not be characterized by right-wing critics as lackeys of Moscow's Communist regime.

Neier became a friend of Jacobo Timerman, the Argentine newspaper publisher who was imprisoned and tortured by the military in the late 1970s, before he was finally exiled. Timerman's memoir *Prisoner Without a Name, Cell Without a Number* remains one of the most important books published during the time of the generals. It is also a terrifying account of one man's struggle to retain his humanity under torture.

Americas Watch distinguished itself from other organizations engaged in the struggle for human rights by its detailed and careful documentation of what it monitored. Its staff travelled to bombed Salvadoran villages in order to document that the government was murdering peasant farmers because they could have been in a position to help the rebels.

In Nicaragua, they exposed massacres by both the Sandinistas and the US-sponsored contras. They used field researchers in conflict zones to expose the CIA's tactics in US government-sponsored disappearances, murder, and torture. As Neier says, the research provided the truth. "We disputed them [the US government's representatives] on the facts."

Neier himself travelled to all the countries investigated by Americas Watch, and occasionally intervened directly in the fate of those arrested. He was, according to several colleagues, fearless.

He pioneered the need to hold officials accountable for acts committed by a government who paid their wages. Justice finally reached the military, including the former director of the secret police, in Chile and, although it was slow in arriving, it also reached the military in Argentina. Critics of the process, including Henry Kissinger and Margaret Thatcher, objected to prosecutions of rightist government leaders and their supporters, while those on the left were unchallenged. Neier insists that human rights investigations were politically even-handed.

In 1984, he travelled to Poland to carry messages of encouragement and much-needed funds for members of the anti-Communist resistance. Although martial law had just been lifted the year before, it was hardly the best time for tourism. Nevertheless, Neier took his wife, Yvette, to demonstrate his genuine interest in sightseeing.

He met with some of the intellectuals who supported Solidarity, the trade union led by Lech Walesa, and carried messages and cash from the West. Konstanty (Kostek) Gebert remembers the rather awkward evening when the Neiers arrived unannounced, and he almost lit a cigarette that contained a hidden message the Neiers had brought from Solidarity while the couple patiently listened to his story about the revival of the Jewish community in Warsaw.

In 1985, Bernstein, Schell, and Neier established Asia Watch, possibly as a result of the Dalai Lama's indirect approach to Neier proposing a visit to Tibet. Although the Chinese government refused to issue the necessary visas, Tibet became a major focus for the new foundation.

Africa Watch and Middle East Watch, with a $3.5 million grant from the MacArthur Foundation, followed. By the time the various bureaus were in place, Human Rights Watch, the umbrella organization, had almost founded itself. It was the first international organization to call for the banning of landmines.

Neier became an advocate of transnational justice in the eighties when the Argentine military gave themselves a full amnesty for the kidnappings, rapes, murders, and subsequent cover-up that had taken place in the late seventies. He was instrumental in the creation of the International Criminal Tribunal for the Former Yugoslavia. Ken Roth, his successor at Human Rights Watch, credits Neier with setting up the methodology that is still Human Rights Watch's hallmark: detailed, thorough investigations, research, and the "use of objective fact."[2]

Roth was hired by Neier and says he learned all he knows from working for him. A thin, bespectacled, agile man, he is the perfect opposite to Neier's more reserved personality. He has been in all the trouble spots of the past twenty or so years: Bosnia, Ivory Coast, Kenya, the Congo, and Rwanda. Like his former boss, he has great confidence in the International Criminal Court and, where it hasn't been able to assert itself, in naming and shaming the perpetrators.

To underline his even-handed approach to rights violations, Neier went to Cuba in 1988 and visited several jails where political prisoners were held. He had gained the friendship and confidence of Jorge Valls, who had served "twenty years and forty days"[3] in one of those jails for peacefully protesting Fidel Castro's violations of human rights. Neier helped expose the forced "re-education" methods and the long, solitary confinements in cramped quarters. He realized later that several dissenters whom he had met were harassed by police after his visit.

In 1992 President George H. W. Bush signed the Torture Victims Protection Act, a piece of legislation that provides civil remedies in countries other than those where the tortures occurred.

Neier first met Soros in 1979. Soros agreed to fund Neier's efforts to bring academics from eastern Europe to the United States as visiting scholars. During the next fifteen years, about 3,000 writers, journalists, scientists, and historians came to the West. In the process, many of them formed lasting relationships that would later help their countries, institutions, journals, and universities. Soros attended some of Neier's weekly conferences in New York and became a supporter of Human Rights Watch. What sealed their partnership, Neier recalled, was Soros's immediate commitment of $50 million for Bosnia. The two men shared a revulsion to crimes committed in the name of nationalism or racism. They had both known National Socialism.

When Neier went to Sarajevo in 1993, he argued with British General Michael Rose over Rose's decision to blame both sides of the conflict equally when the citizens of Sarajevo were hunted from the hills by the Serbian army. The preposterous idea that the Bosnians were shelling themselves, Neier told me, suited the British politics of non-intervention, just as ignoring Canadian General Roméo Dallaire's warning about Rwanda had served President Clinton's wish to stay out of the conflict in Africa.

It is interesting that Rose, in his own book, *Fighting for Peace*, had a completely different view of his encounter with Neier and Neier's colleague, "the shadowy" Fred Cuny. Rose's lasting first impression of Neier was that the man was "a zealot," who had no interest in listening to Rose's take on what the UN mission should be about. As for Cuny, he was "an ex-US Marine Corps officer … straight out of a Graham Greene novel." Rose relished throwing them out of his office.

Neier's often-repeated example of expediency over morality includes the meeting on October 14, 1944, of twenty-three men and women from the International Red Cross. They already knew about the Nazis' systematic mass murder of Jews and gypsies, but they decided to keep silent because they believed their primary responsibility was for prisoners of war, not civilians.

What happened in Sarajevo was another example of expediency over morality or politics over simple humanity. Two hundred thousand people had been killed and many, many more wounded when Neier went there to see the horror for himself. Adding to General Rose's obdurate resistance to reality, the commander of the French troops ordered his men to spotlight those who tried to escape, thus making it easier to kill them. As for Cuny, he installed the Soros-funded water-system that saved citizens from Serbian sniper-fire every time they ventured out for water.

Neier joined George Soros in 1993 and served as president of the Open Society Institute, later renamed Open Society Foundations, until June 2012. His arrival presaged an immediate increase in the foundations' focus on human rights. The foundations began to engage lawyers and researchers worldwide to try to ensure that those responsible for human rights violations on a grand scale were forced to account for their actions in the courts of justice, whether in their own countries or in the International Criminal Court in The Hague.

It was Neier who defined the seven conditions for an open society, the conditions that helped establish the aims of the network of foundations that he managed for Soros. The conditions, according to Soros in *Open Society: Reforming Global Capitalism*, are regular, free, and fair elections; free and pluralistic media; the rule of law upheld by an independent judiciary; constitutional protection for minority rights; a market economy that respects property rights and provides opportunities and a safety net for the disadvantaged; a commitment to the peaceful resolution of conflicts; and laws that are enforced to curb corruption.

Needless to say, no country I can think of demonstrates all of these characteristics, but they do provide something to strive for, even in wartime and even when one side feels justified in inflicting pain on the other.

During his tenure, Open Society spent more than $1 billion promoting democracy in eastern Europe and the remnants of the Soviet Union; approximately another $1 billion in Russia; and about $2 billion to defend human rights in countries where they are not valued by governments or warring factions trying to grab power. For example, Open Society spent about $200 million to advance the rights of the Roma in Europe. Then Soros and Neier began to focus on the United States and what they viewed as a need to repair democracy.

On Neier's watch, Open Society spent more than $1 billion to promote a variety of social initiatives, including reforming a criminal justice system that discriminates against blacks, promoting alternatives to jail sentences for petty crimes, ending the war on drugs, stopping the arrest and torture of terror suspects, and promoting the right to die. They spent almost $2 billion on educational projects, the Central European University in Budapest, Open Society Fellowships, public health, promoting reproductive rights, setting up legal services to serve poor regional organizations, and the mushrooming civil rights efforts in Asia, Africa, and the Middle East. Open Society's most substantial spending during the period from 2011 to 2014 was on its Justice Initiative.

I first met Neier at Open Society's Fifty-Ninth Street offices in January 2012, a year before their move to new premises and five months before Neier's retirement. The old offices were rather spartan, a rabbit warren of small spaces with low white dividers. The executives fared somewhat better, with narrow windows and enough room for one visitor, but they exhibited a lack of interest in physical surroundings. Neier's corner office had a large bookcase, two sets of windows, a desk, a few chairs, a sofa, and a low coffee table.

Gara LaMarche, who worked for Neier at both Human Rights Watch and at Open Society, described him as "penetrating, amazingly smart, but a lot of people found him intimidating. He is not one for small talk and many, including a lot he regards very highly, don't know where they stand with him." Now, Neier seemed distanced rather than intimidating. It was as if he was concerned with something else, somewhere else, and its prospect was discomforting. Courteous, soft spoken, patient, he tended to avoid continuous eye contact, either out of politeness or boredom with recounting the past.

Much had changed during his eighteen years, but not the twin evils of human misery and the murder of innocents. In the United States, the police were still routinely stopping and frisking black men and the vast prison population was still disproportionately black. It is difficult to enforce equal justice when bail is set too high for the poor. While the United Nations has condemned atrocities and attacks on civilians during armed conflicts, they have continued unabated. The Geneva Conventions did nothing to diminish the misery of civilians in war zones. Neier pointed to Rwanda, Kenya, Mali, the Central African Republic, and the unsuccessful, delayed court proceedings in Cambodia. The justice system had delayed prosecutions for so long that most of the perpetrators were either dead or about to die.

Neier admitted that even as he was getting ready to vacate this office, he was still not sure of all the Open Society activities that cascade around the world. The foundations have myriad operations. Some are run in their own countries (e.g., Poland's Batory Foundation) while others are managed from the New York offices. The Washington Office is an advocacy centre that tries to influence the US government's policies, both on domestic and international issues (for example, criminal justice reform in the US and the future of girls and women in Afghanistan).

Little wonder that Neier couldn't keep track of it all. I doubt whether his replacement, Chris Stone, will be able to figure out what everyone is doing in the OSF's spanking new offices either, let alone everywhere else its tentacles reach.

A great deal has happened since Neier took part in antiwar marches in the sixties, and a great deal has changed since he joined the Open Society Foundations. But there is still a long way to go.

Terror has remained a favoured route to power. As he told an audience in 2012, "it is difficult to deter by conventional methods" terrorists who are willing to kill themselves in order to inflict harm on those with whom they have no quarrel.

What, if any good, have the international agreements done? What possible use can it be to have new institutions, such as the International Criminal Court in The Hague, if atrocities continue as they always have?

Neier believed, he said, that the threat of having to answer for past deeds at the International Criminal Court created some concern among perpetrators, but it is not enough. "We must find a way to combat their justifications for the killing of civilians."[4] The terrorists' own sense of victimhood does not give them the right to kill innocent people. "We need a consistent moral condemnation of the murder of civilians."

Neier believes that most of the 800,000 deaths in Rwanda could have been prevented if the UN had been willing to intervene. But President Clinton was concerned about the elections and a repeat of the horror of Mogadishu: US servicemen butchered in a faraway land, defending unfamiliar people who did not welcome them. "I believe," he said, "that at those crucial times, those in leadership positions must speak up for civilians."

Both Soros and Neier had been loud opponents of President Bush's policy of US exceptionalism. They argued that no leader should be able determine that the Geneva Conventions do not apply to them. It is impossible to take the moral high ground when a country is unwilling to follow the rules of civilized behaviour.

Neier still espouses the unbridled right to free speech in the United

States, but he is less ready to support the Rwandan radio hosts who extolled the atrocities in their country or the media in Yugoslavia in the 1990s that promoted ethnic cleansing. So when does free speech become a criminal offence? In *Taking Liberties*, Neier goes to some length to explain what he believes are acceptable limits on free speech, but it seems the division is mainly one of geography and degree. In some cases, one person's freedom to express his views can impinge on the rights of others.

Neier told me that while he is somewhat disappointed in the International Criminal Court's prosecutions, at least there are prosecutions and the fact that 121 countries have signed on to the ICC shows that, despite all the horror we see in the world, there is still some desire for justice. He also talked about the failure of truth commissions. Although Neier is widely credited with pushing through funds for South Africa's Truth and Reconciliation Commission, he said it had worked only because of Nelson Mandela's personal involvement. A traditional legal approach could have caused a civil war.

Rwanda's traditional proceedings where individuals must admit to their participation in the killings is neither transparent, nor satisfying to the victims, but it does create an awareness and may serve to prevent a recurrence. It may have worked in Peru, and it definitely worked in Guatemala. Neier travelled to Guatemala several times during General Montt's rule. He listened to harrowing stories of abuse and appalling tales of the extermination of entire villages. Some witnesses he listened to were later killed. The fact that US President Reagan supported the Montt regime and claimed that his terrible human rights record was exaggerated helped provide an acceptable face for the killers.

In March 2013, José Efrain Rios Montt was tried for genocide. It was a historically important charge, Neier said, as this was the first time a head of state had been tried in his own country on such charges. The eighty-six-year-old former president was convicted of overseeing a campaign of disappearances, massacres, forced displacement, torture, rape, and sexual assaults directed against the Mayan Ixil community, who were suspected of supporting Communist rebels. He was sentenced to eighty years in prison, a term he was rather unlikely to endure. Strangely, the verdict was set aside by the country's constitutional court. The judges claimed that due process had been violated by the three judges presiding over the trial. Even more surprising, given the nature of the charges, the head of military intelligence during the Montt regime, Mauricio Rodriguez Sanchez, was acquitted.

"The trouble is," Neier said, "that truth commissions do not resolve individual responsibility. All they can do is to define the tragedy."

"And allow people to move on with their lives?" I asked.

"Sometimes."[5]

Neier was not interested in talking about his legacy, but he was proud of having been the first to support Aung San Suu Kyi, the Burmese politician and Nobel Prize winner. He was pleased with President Ellen Johnson Sirleaf's democratic reforms in Sierra Leone. While it may not seem like a natural progression from Eastern Europe to South Asia, the Middle East, and sub-Saharan Africa, these countries represented opportunities to expand Open Society's influence and to force issues of democracy, entrepreneurship, and equal rights under the law. Sadly, as Freedom House has reported, the twenty-first century has not shown signs that democracy is gaining impetus. Several European countries have reverted to authoritarianism, populist far-right parties are gaining support, the European Union is on the edge of a precipice, Ukraine is burning, Russia is flexing its muscles, both in Europe and in Syria, and the United States is no longer leading nor providing a shining example to others. It launched a losing war in Iraq, allowed its CIA operatives to detain and torture suspects and, President Obama's campaign promises to the contrary, is still detaining prisoners in Guantánamo.

"We still have a foundation in Afghanistan, but it is not easy to operate there. Our people believe that the only way to settle the conflict is to make a deal with the Taliban, but we are afraid of what we would have to give up." Neier mentioned the judicial system and women's rights, as if either of these gains was still there to fight for. "I don't want to oppose a peace process, but I am afraid for Afghans."[6] He talked of Nader Naderi, who had been the Human Rights Commissioner in Afghanistan until he was sacked by President Hamid Karzai in 2010. Naderi had repeatedly voiced his concerns about the unlikelihood of free and fair elections.

As the events of the Arab Spring unfolded, there were moments of hope for what Neier believed was a universal yearning for human rights and justice. But it was, he said, too soon to know how those twin desires would unfold in Egypt and Tunisia. The Egyptian military has substantial financial interests in the region, which probably means that massive change is unlikely. Meanwhile, the director of Open Society's Egyptian office now lives in Paris.

"I have not, personally, assessed the role of Islamist parties, but I am told they are not opposed to democracy," Neier said.

I wondered who on earth had told him that.

In Libya, there were already signs that the new government was as willing to engage in torture as the old one under Muammar Gaddafi had been. "Violent revolutions are not usually a good way to develop an open society. People who have engaged in violence tend to end up on top," Neier observed. At the end of 2014, there was anarchy in Libya. Syria had been devastated by civil war and was now in the grip of ISIS. To celebrate his being honoured with the International Rescue Committee's Freedom Award in November, 2013, Soros pledged $1 million for humanitarian aid in Syria. He blamed both the government and the rebels for denying both food and warmth to the beleaguered civilian population.

Despite Soros's statements that the regime in Iraq is doomed to fail, Neier said Iraq is not in Open Society's sights. "We felt we would have little influence. I didn't want to put our staff at risk ..."

Lawyer and refugee advocate Arthur Helton, a friend of Neier, was killed in 2003 in Baghdad's Canal Hotel. He had been a member of the Lawyers Committee for Human Rights.

"Sometimes I think there is an inverse relationship between aid and improvement in people's lives," Neier told me. That's quite an admission from a man who has spent most of his life in the aid business.

WHEN I RETURNED in June 2012, Neier was reading the top sheet in a thin sheaf that I assumed was a manuscript. His book, *International Human Rights Movement: A History*, was published in 2012 by Princeton University Press. It weighs in at 380 pages of densely written prose, delivering on the promise of the title. Its central thesis is that the recognition of human rights — the essential focus on morality when dealing with human beings in all cases, in all countries — must be promoted, fought, and sometimes died for by non-governmental activists, rather than by governments and their agencies. It is through the actions of these disparate, often disorganized, hard-working visionaries that what little has been achieved has been achieved at all. Their successes include the establishment of international law and institutions that may have serious shortcomings, but at least they have come into being. The impunity with which countries such as Brazil and Nigeria have practised police violence and brutal government repression is no longer as easily reached as it was at the beginning of the 1900s.

Neier writes with some gusto about the international outrage at the actions of Augusto Pinochet and his armed forces; with disgust about President Richard Nixon's support for those actions; and with satisfaction that Nixon was ousted from the White House in 1974.

What is mostly missing from the book is Neier's personal role in the movement he helped create. His emotions are as well hidden in the book as they are in person. His desk was clean, his book shelves in order, his parting smile in place.

As for regrets, there may be only one. Neier seems to be still haunted by his colleague Fred Cuny's gruesome death in Chechnya. Cuny, an adventurous spirit and supporter of Neier's human rights work, went to Chechnya to broker some sort of peace between the Russian forces and the Chechen rebels — at least until civilians could be removed from the line of fire. The last call Cuny made was to Neier, and Neier agreed to the mission. "If he had told me something specific, like [he was] seeing Dudayev, I would have said, 'No way,' but I restrained myself in dealing with someone who was much my better in terms of the capacity to deal with these kinds of situations."[7]

Cuny was captured, probably tortured, and certainly killed by either a Chechen warlord, or a Russian commander.

Human rights is dangerous work and others, too, have died in its pursuit, but it is Cuny's death that Neier seems to regret most profoundly.

"My legacy," he said when I asked again, "is that I have tried to play a role in helping young people in human rights work."

The American Civil Liberties Union and Human Rights Watch have set up an Aryeh Neier fellowship for initiatives to strengthen human rights in the United States. In 2010, George Soros gave $100 million ($10 million a year over ten years) to Human Rights Watch.

The man himself now occupies a smaller office on the third floor of Open Society's new premises.

FIVE

The Hub in New York

The Open Society Foundations' mission is to "work to build vibrant and tolerant democracies whose governments are accountable to their citizens." Their website explains that they "seek to strengthen the rule of law; respect for human rights, minorities, and a diversity of opinions; democratically elected governments; and a civil society that helps keep government power in check." They help shape "public policies that assure greater fairness in political, legal, and economic systems and safeguard fundamental rights." In addition, they advance the causes of justice, education, public health, and independent media and build alliances to counter corruption worldwide.

Their core values include focusing on righting inequalities, responding to critical threats to open society, and respecting diverse opinions. It's a huge mandate, one with long arms and a broad reach that has meant setting up separate groups to deal with separate issues and some semi-independent entities in a variety of countries.

The foundations have a complicated organizational structure, likely because they grew organically rather than according to a plan. It would appear that Open Society responded to needs and ideas as they arose by hiring highly intelligent and exceptionally well-educated people who took on whatever responsibilities they were handed.

The foundations operate twenty-one programs and an astonishing array of sub-programs. There are twenty-three boards, including the Open Society Global Board, and thirty-nine offices and foundations spread out around the world. Many of these, such as the Stefan Batory Foundation in Poland, the Open Society Foundation–London, the OSI Baltimore, and the International Renaissance Foundation in Ukraine, have their own boards and advisory boards.

To complicate matters further, each Open Society program works on a range of issues across several regions. The Human Rights Initiative, for instance, works on governance, rights and justice, disability rights, discrimination, and LGBTI-related questions and spreads its wings over Africa, Asia, Europe, Latin America, the Caribbean, and the Middle East. The Eurasia Program works to deepen civil society and uphold human rights in places as far apart as Armenia, Moldova, Azerbaijan, Turkmenistan, and Georgia. This program's tasks also include combating corruption, strengthening independent media, and creating platforms for debate. The list of philanthropies on the foundations' website extends to five hundred pages. To explore them all would not be practical, so I have focused here on a few key areas.

Open Society's Global Board includes Robert Soros, George's oldest son. Robert is also president and deputy chairman of the $28 billion Soros Fund Management. Like his father, Robert is part of the Hillary Clinton Super PAC and donates to the arts and liberal causes. Two other sons, Jonathan and Alexander, are on the Advisory Board, as is George's daughter, Andrea Soros Colombel. Jonathan is CEO of the investment firm JS Capital Management LLC and founder of Friends of Democracy, a Super PAC that supports candidates who favour limits on big money in US politics — all of which points to him being a chip off the old block. (Total spending on the 2014 mid-term Senate race topped $4 billion,[1] about $100 million in Georgia alone. Ironically, Jonathan has spent millions combating excessive spending in campaigns.) Alexander, still studying for his doctorate, runs the Alexander Soros Foundation, which supports human rights, social justice, and education — another chip off the old block. No slouch herself, Andrea is founder and board chair of the Acumen Fund and president of the Trace Foundation.

In 2013, the foundations collectively spent $873,344,000. That does not include OSI-Zug, Soros's Switzerland-based foundation.[2] It's interesting to note that OSI-Zug seems to have spent about £11 million on OSF causes and supported OSF-London with £17 million in 2010.[3]

TO TRY TO MAKE some sense of all this activity, I ventured into Open Society's New York City offices. My first visit was in the autumn of 2011. At that time, most of the foundations' senior people and their assistants were at 400 Fifty-Ninth Street, just behind Columbus Circle, not far from the glitzy towers lining Central Park West. I have visited several times since, although I have been to their new offices on 224 West Fifty-Seventh Street only twice. I met most of the senior people who work in these offices and direct the foundations' funds.

It is interesting to observe that the man who said he wanted no bureaucracy, who believed that a small, nimble organization was the best way to achieve a seamless transfer of money directly to the people who most needed it, has ended up with a behemoth that employs more than a thousand people, about four hundred of them in this office alone. Soros, who declared he did not believe in institutions, has built one in the heart of New York with myriad offshoots in other cities and other countries.

Administration cost a mere $97,274,000 in 2013. The Washington Office accounted for $5 million of that, about the same amount that the organization spends on communications. Strangely, Central European University weighs in at only $451,000, while its draw from its Endowment Funds is a healthy €39 million.[4]

It is difficult to get an exact count of employees, as no one seems to know all of the people in all of the places where Open Society and its affiliates manage their myriad programs. Even Soros himself has admitted that he cannot give "a proper accounting of the far-reaching and varied activities … because I am not aware of them all." In the past, there were other offices in other parts of New York, but all the New York staff were united at 224 West Fifty-Seventh Street (between Broadway and Seventh Avenue) in early 2013.

In *Underwriting Democracy*, Soros set out how he would avoid the kind of structure that characterized the Ford Foundation. His aim, he said, was "not to be visible at all." He wanted to avoid turning recipients into "objects of charity." He said he was determined to "avoid a centralized structure at all costs," as innovative ideas are generated from the ground up, not from the top.

When Soros's charitable works began, there were just three or four people in a corner of his business office, as Liz Lorant remembered.[5] Lorant, who was born in Hungary and came to the United States in 1956, was the second employee. It was 1984, and George wanted to start something in Hungary. "At first there was just a nutrition program for kids," she recalls, then an early childhood education program that George Soros called "two plus six."

Lorant had written a page and a half on how a child's chances of developing thinking skills would be helped by starting some critical thinking at age two. She called it "Step-by-Step."

"George sat with his feet up on the table, glanced at the piece of paper and he said I must spend $100 million on this. It was the strangest thing." But, Lorant says, it worked brilliantly in Hungary where the prototype was designed, then it rolled out across thirty-one countries. Now the program operates in about 130 countries, including Mongolia, Azerbaijan, and Georgia, and has its own corporate structure, a business plan, and a head office in Europe.

Its list of objectives includes "child centred education; encouraging the democratic process in children and adults; providing children opportunities for creative expression; advocating support for children with special needs," and so on. "George had great instinct for projects," Lorant says.

She has not visited Open Society's new offices, but if she did I'm sure she would be amazed at the rabbit warren of small spaces marked by red and white dividers. There are a few status offices for meetings along the outside walls and, while I didn't count the windows, there is no doubt that a greater number of windows denotes greater importance, just as it does in government buildings, law firms, and banks. The people who interested me most were the ones with the windows, as they are likely to deliver Soros's legacy.

Aryeh Neier, president emeritus, had an office with two sets of windows. It's the least they could do for a man who directed Soros's funds for almost twenty years.

Leonard Benardo, who was "responsible for," among other places, Russia, Hungary, the Baltics, Poland, and Ukraine, had only one window. His office was narrow and had paper piles on every surface. He was in a hurry, his longish hair flapping as he dashed in and out his door, arranging meetings with people from India and China. (Will he inherit another country?)

He was working for OSF in Russia when the foundation's offices were closed. "The nineties were humiliating for Russians. There was anarchy. Fragmentation. Disarray. People were disoriented. Oligarchs running amok. The state had collapsed. Putin offered stability — *stability* was his watchword." Benardo said all this in between answering his phone.

He was not excited by the 2011 demonstrations in Russia, but the fact that anyone at all showed up to protest gave him reason to pause. "Solidarity is very unusual there. Citizens are atomized."

He dashed out to welcome some people from the "Fellowship Program" and mentioned his great admiration for Professor Andrew Nathan, an expert on Chinese politics and foreign policy. Nathan is, apparently, the man I would want to talk to if I was planning to open an NGO in China.

During the summer of 2012, Benardo invited me to lunch at an Italian restaurant near the old office. Apart from being in too much of a hurry to enjoy his food, he seemed a lot more relaxed. He talked about how Russian businessman Mikhail Khodorkovsky's arrest and trial had affected Soros, noting that it was "a watershed moment for him." He hadn't anticipated that Putin would make such a move. Nor, it seems, had Benardo anticipated the state's invasion of the foundation's offices there, nor the impunity with which the government is able to act against anyone considered an enemy — a category that includes most Western NGOs.

Anthony Richter, another important member of Open Society's senior management, has been with the foundations since 1988. "I was special advisor to George Soros," he says with some pride. He used to be head of the Soros Foundation in the Soviet Union. He was pleased to tell me he had opened more than twenty offices: Latvia, Lithuania, Estonia, Belarus, Ukraine, Mongolia, Turkey … the names rolled off his tongue like a litany. At the time of our interview, he was the director of the Middle East and North Africa Initiatives and had overall responsibility for the Arab region as well as for Afghanistan and Pakistan. He started Revenue Watch and chaired the governing board of the Revenue Watch Institute. He speaks Russian, French, and Persian, it says on his blog. Not Farsi, Persian.

He has closely cropped hair, a short, trimmed beard, and glasses. He had recently come back from Tajikistan, Turkmenistan, and Kyrgyzstan, where President Roza Otunbayeva, he hoped, might still be a friend. (By the time I wrote this, Otunbayeva was no longer president and the "beacon of democracy in Kyrgyzstan," as the *Daily Telegraph* wrote, "may have been staunched.") In November 2014, Soros met with Kyrgyz head of state Almazbek Atambayev to discuss the foundations' work in education, health, and culture. Open Society's spending in Kyrgyzstan was $5 million in 2013, and in Kazakhstan a little more than $4 million.

Martha Loerke runs the extensive scholarship program, the current incarnation of the old one that started back in the 1980s when Soros was handing out educational opportunities to promising youngsters behind the Iron Curtain. She began going to the USSR in the summer of 1987 and travelled to most parts of the country to gather applicants for about 13,000 scholarships. At the time, the non-profit world considered Soros's approach to philanthropy "a bit scattershot — not in motives, but in implementation." Not so any more, she said.

A striking woman with shoulder-length brown-grey hair, Loerke has been managing scholarships for more than twenty-five years. Open Society has handed out thousands of scholarships in the former Soviet Union, eastern Europe, the Middle East, Africa, the Balkans, Sierra Leone, Mozambique, and to refugees from Burma. The foundations spent $21,225 million on scholarships in 2013.

"I think we changed people's lives," she said. "Soros has always been interested in power for the individual, and scholarships have empowered young people who will be the future of their countries."

I met Mike Hall on my first visit to the old offices, where he greeted me with an open smile and a strong handshake. Hall has a degree from Harvard, but he has also studied in Tashkent. He is the regional director for the Caucasus region and Central Asia. He is young and earnest, probably a requirement for managing thirty-seven foundations in seven contentious "stans." It's not very fertile ground for open societies. These countries have horrific human rights records, are steeped in corruption, and closed to most Western approaches. Uzbekistan routinely uses forced child labour in the cotton fields, where conditions are dangerous and unrewarded. The government closes elementary and secondary schools and universities to make sure the children are available for work. Transparency International ranked Uzbekistan 170th for corruption in a field of only 178.

Hall writes papers about the region, which he believes is changing. He advocates for human rights monitoring, legal reforms, Revenue Watch interventions, Transparency International standards, and fewer layers of complications within Open Society's various programs. He has tried to see what roles could be played in Georgia, where the broadcast media are controlled and the judicial system is compromised, and in Kazakhstan where the oil boom has not offered opportunities for people yearning for good schools, reasonable healthcare, and an honest police force.

For reasons I couldn't fathom, Mike Hall managed to seem cheerful about his work.

When I first visited Open Society, Abdul Tejan Cole's office was along the same wall as Benardo's and was equally narrow, although slightly less cluttered. When I met Cole, he was the regional director for Africa. Before being hired by Open Society, he had been an attorney for the Special Court of Sierra Leone, president of the Sierra Leone Bar Association, head of the Anti-Corruption Commission from 2007 to 2010, and board chair for OSI West Africa. He has a long list of degrees and honours. His first postgraduate degree was an MA in shipping law, which is relevant because Sierra Leone has one of the best harbours in the world.

Cole is a slim black man with an open smile and light-framed glasses. He wore a white open-necked shirt and a dark suit. "I was in Sierra Leone when it was booming," he said. "The wealthiest country in the region. We were self-sufficient. Things started changing in the eighties — massive corruption, misappropriation of resources, diamonds, coffee, iron ore ... all used to fund the civil war of the nineties." He showed me *Prosecuting Heads of State*, a book that includes one of his essays.

He is a great believer in establishing the rule of law and keeping it out of the hands of governments. His father was a criminal lawyer, his aunts are lawyers, and one aunt is the chief justice of Sierra Leone.

"For a while," he said, "the war was easy to ignore. My practice was going well." But then he began to take an interest in human rights, supporting people who documented rights abuses by the rebels and publishing the atrocities. It was his sense of outrage that attracted him to Open Society. It is the only organization, he told me, that gives you a budget that can make a difference, and they trust your judgment on how to make the best use of it: "I had $10 million to work a few small miracles." He is proud of the school that he opened in Liberia for girls who had been raped and had children by the rebels. He provided a water supply for a village in Swaziland, and a chicken farm somewhere else: "We gave them opportunities and hope."

The last time I heard from Cole, he had been relocated to Senegal as the executive director for Open Society's West Africa foundation, with a budget of $24.7 million. In 2014, he was plunged into the middle of the Ebola crisis and responsible for the $4 million emergency grant from Open Society to set up a medical centre. In a video message on September 17, he talked of pressuring governments in the region to take a more coherent approach to organizing their response to the devastating virus, and he applauded fellow Africans who are coming back to help their countries in times of crisis.

His neat black suit had been exchanged for a shiny, flowing African gown of gold and light blue thread. He had come home.

The Human Rights Initiative had by far the biggest budget in 2014.[6] Its director is Emily Martinez, who holds both an MA and a BS. She has worked for Open Society on LGBTI rights and the rights of criminal defendants. She was the director of Human Rights and Governance during the foundations' early days in Budapest, promoting law and accountable governments in eastern Europe and the Soviet Union.

Tawanda Mutasah, formerly of the High Court of Zimbabwe, was the director of transnational or "network programs" for Open Society. The foundation calls them "network programs" because they are mostly thematic in nature — "arts and culture," "education," "human rights," and "public health" — rather than specific to a country or continent.

Mutasah spoke of "violent crime" in Zambia, Namibia, and the Balkans, as though they all had the same common denominator. In his view, violence has no single country. It is generic. He talked of the Justice Initiative and the International Women's Program, and of "public health" with a budget of close to $50 million. That seemed like a great deal of money to me, but Mutasah said they have all had to pull back to stay within their budgets.

He was charming — formal but friendly. His hands stretched to embrace a large number of issues or geographic areas; then his palms came together to hold all the thoughts he was trying to express. His fingers reached around grant-making, trying to use money to help individuals.

Mutasah still keeps alive the hope for a democratic society in his homeland of Zimbabwe. He was a student leader in a country ruled by a dictator who "saw students as his enemies and our demonstrations as challenges to his power." He was arrested, handcuffed, beaten, and finally hospitalized. His family was threatened. To this day, he will not sit with his back to a door, instinctively recoiling at the possibility of another attack.

If the regime's intent was to deter him, it failed. He is still fighting for all the beliefs he held as a student. "This job," he says, "is ideal. I help to keep courage alive in places where there is little reason for hope. In Zimbabwe, we need to show that the world is still watching, that there is no such thing as impunity."

He worked in South Africa for the international coalition to establish the International Criminal Court in The Hague. He was delighted to see Chile's General Pinochet arrested, Liberia's Charles Taylor tried, and the warlords of the Congo shown that justice is not merely another Western concept.

He talked of the Roma programs, the effort to politicize Roma leaders, to engage them in advocacy, and to help them make the most of those

EU funds that have such a tough time reaching them. He described the "Roma pride" camps and the struggle to reduce prejudice. But he is not so naïve as to think that the trumpeting EU announcements around the Decade of Roma Inclusion have made much difference in the lives of average Roma families in eastern Europe. Both the European Union and Open Society Foundations have a long way to go.

He handed me an Open Society brochure on the International Women's Program: equality and justice under the rule of law. The program is so broad-ranging that it's difficult to see how it can be effective in its aims to prevent violence, pursue justice, and push leadership roles for women.

Mutasah is no longer head of "network programs." It seems that under the leadership of Open Society's new president Chris Stone, all programs will return to their roots in other places.

"Tawanda," said Stone, "has gone back to study. He will have a new job when he returns." Instead, he is now Senior Director for Law and Policy at Amnesty International.

When I last saw him, Stewart Paperin was executive vice president of Open Society Foundations and president of the Soros Economic Development Fund. His corner office had two wide views of the buildings across the street, and his spacious quarters looked more like a corporate office than the crammed areas occupied by other senior staff. He is a genial man with a strong handshake, an open smile, and expansive gestures. He said his mandate was to oversee twenty-nine core foundations from Haiti to Turkey, Pakistan to Senegal. Although there is no office in China, he directs a China initiative with direct grants to individuals and institutions.

The Soros Economic Development Fund, with assets of about $250 million, has grown from a modest investment of $50 million. The fund is outside of Open Society's official borders. It operates in "post-conflict countries where it can provide both a social benefit and a return on the fund's investment." For example, Leapfrog in Africa invests in micro insurance policies. In Sierra Leone, there is a refrigerated truck business, and in Liberia the focus is on housing. "But every time we decide on a new initiative," he says, "it must be viewed through a human rights lens." The housing plans for South Africans, for example, had to serve the needy. Now 300,000 homes attest to the success of the investment. Business has been exceptionally good.

The fund has three offices, but employs only fifteen people, according to its last available annual report.

On the side, Paperin also negotiated the thirty-one-year lease for Open Society Foundations' new office space. He sees himself as one-third businessman (he used to be a financial executive), one-third diplomat, and one-third humanitarian. As for Soros, "I always give him my best advice. Sometimes he doesn't like it, but when I tell him the emperor has no clothes he listens." Unlike some others around Soros, Paperin is not afraid to be critical.

Surprisingly, he does not view Open Society's work in Russia as a failure. Thirty Russian universities are connected to the Internet thanks to Soros. Those computers were all provided by the foundation. This is part of the Soros legacy, as is Soros's role in saving Sarajevo, reforming the criminal justice system in the United States, and working to decriminalize drug use.

Paperin does not list saving Europe as one of Soros's grand legacy projects. "They will not listen to him. George has no public relations strengths. He fails to sympathize with politicians and they, overall, ignore him."

James Goldston is the executive director of Open Society's Justice Initiative. He has a tiny office, but lots of assistants who kept calling him to attend to urgent matters. He travels constantly and seemed genuinely surprised by my writing a book about Open Society. Who would be interested, he wondered.

His colleague Laura Silber, who is Open Society's director of Public Affairs, used to be a journalist for the *Financial Times*. She was sympathetic to my efforts to make sense of the foundations' structure, but she remained wary, in case I took something that she said out of context. In the new building she no longer has an office. She uses one of the open spaces, as does her new boss, Chris Stone.

Kasia Malinowska-Sempruch is director of the Global Drug Policy Program. Before joining Open Society, she worked for the United Nations on HIV issues in New York City and in Warsaw. She managed programs on harm reduction, women's health, medical ethics, and drug use. She has written numerous studies and papers on topics related to her work. Like most of the foundations' senior people, she has a graduate degree.

The Independent Journalism Program is run out of London. Its new director, appointed in May 2014, is Maria Teresa Ronderos from Columbia. She will have a budget of $12 million to promote freedom of expression in places where such freedoms are dangerous.

Herb Sturz is the last person I interviewed from the senior management team. Sturz doesn't quite fit the pattern of youngish executives, yet he may be the most interesting person there. More than eighty years old, tall, white-haired, and long-legged, he walks quickly, arms swinging, a man in a hurry. He has a big smile and an even bigger handshake. There is a book about him: *Sturz: A Kind of Genius* by Sam Roberts. The book does not exaggerate. Sturz's passion has always been for underdogs and, judging by all he has achieved, he is some kind of genius.

He has worked with skid-row derelicts in tough neighbourhoods. He managed to convince the New York City police that arresting men and putting them in jail cells was too much paperwork because the same people would always clog the system. He set up an infirmary in the Bowery to serve the homeless and let them be cared for until they felt ready to go back on the street.

He is a former deputy mayor for criminal justice in New York City. While he was chairman of the City Planning Commission under Mayor Ed Koch, he helped restore the glitter to Times Square.

He has worked on bail reform. "Can you get rid of the bail bondsmen who charge people with no money $500 to get out of jail?" he asks. "Can you change the system to allow those who can't afford bail the same privileges that society offers those who have the cash?" Dropping bail in certain cases would free up a lot of jail cells. Is it possible to give law enforcement people more time to do their real jobs? He started the Vera Institute for Justice with eccentric philanthropist Louise Schwitzer, effectively revolutionizing the bail-bond system. And he is so persuasive that he talked a big New York law firm into taking a case pro bono.

The man has more energy than a twenty-year-old. Dancing around his tiny office, grabbing papers and books, asking his secretary for help locating something he thinks I need to see, statistics on the police's stop-and-frisk records for last year: 700,000 people in New York alone. About 90 percent are black and Latino. "It's utterly senseless, isn't it?" he asks me.

If a young black man is found to have a little bit of marijuana in his pocket, he is charged, he pleads guilty, and now he's got a criminal record. How is he supposed to get a job with that?

When I interviewed him, Sturz had been working with the police commissioner to change the system. He likes to include insiders in his appeals to reason, because insiders have the power to change the system they serve.

In late September 2012, the Community Safety Act, a landmark package of legislation, went before New York City Council. It would bring real accountability to the New York Police Department by prohibiting profiling by race, colour, housing status, religion, and sex and protect New Yorkers from unlawful searches. (Such laws already exist in Illinois, West Virginia, and Arkansas.) In August 2013, Judge Shira Scheindlin[7] found that the stop-and-frisk tactics of the NYPD violated the constitutional rights of minorities, and she called for a federal monitor to oversee reforms. "No one should live in fear of being stopped whenever he leaves his home to go about the activities of daily life."

Typically, the press about the new legislation did not mention Herb Sturz. That's just fine with him. He doesn't like or need to take credit, he said. He has discovered during his long life that others who become wedded to causes feel boosted by the credit they receive. Clearly, he doesn't need the boost.

He met George Soros in January 1994. Ten days later, he was in Johannesburg, building houses for people who couldn't afford to build them. There is a photograph of those yellow and white houses on his wall.

In 1998, he created the After-School Corporation, a non-profit organization that helps communities develop after-school programs for urban youth. It was an idea that everyone supported, but no one had an interest in getting off the ground for the kids who most needed it. Herb, who had once worked at a school for troubled children, sold Soros on the idea during a short breakfast. The After-School Corporation was founded with $125 million from Open Society. It is still running, with additional funds from governments, other foundations, and public support.

In 2005, Sturz and his old friend Jack Rosenthal, then president of the New York Times Company Foundation, started ReServe, based on the premise that retirees — such as themselves — would gladly provide their skills at non-profit and public agencies, if the opportunities existed. By the time I met Sturz, ReServe had placed more than a thousand individuals, but Sturz was not yet happy with the results. More, much more should be done, and yes, why not open an office in Canada?

I don't think Herb Sturz collected a salary for his work at Open Society. He seemed uninterested in personal enrichment. He was excited by the potential for change that his every remaining hour could bring, and I expect to find another bagful of initiatives he is getting his hands around the next time I meet him in New York.

SIX

The Legalist

Although he would disagree with the contention that he has replaced Aryeh Neier, Christopher Stone[1] is the new president of the Open Society Foundations. "I am succeeding Aryeh in a different role," he said. That role includes "institutionalizing" Open Society's political and agile philanthropy. He is readying the foundations for the time when George Soros will no longer be there to lead the way. His kind of "opportunistic" assistance is easy to do on a small scale, but harder with an organization the size that his foundation has become.

Nevertheless, Stone is determined to maintain the spirit of Soros's philanthropy. He is returning to the roots or the beginnings of the foundations: working on the basis of local knowledge rather than top-down management. He said it was important to simplify the structure because it had become too complicated as it grew. That ambition fits with Soros's own view that Open Society needs to be "streamlined." He has eliminated the functions headed by Tawanda Mutasah. "That office does not exist any more," he told me very cheerfully.

In photographs, Stone seems much more casual than Neier because he presents himself without a jacket and sports soft-coloured, wide ties. He is fifty-six-years old and has an easy smile, a high forehead with a distinctive line between his eyes. He wore a healthy tan, although we spoke in 2014 in the middle of winter. That was surprising, given that his flight schedules would not have permitted much time for being oudoors. He has visited most of the foundations' widely flung offices since he joined Open Society in the summer of 2012. Early on, he declared that his focus would be on human rights (as was Aryeh Neier's). "Today, commitments to human rights are under pressure everywhere," he said in June 2013. "Commitments are postponed or abandoned, defenders of rights are attacked." He promised that Open Society, under his leadership, would not compromise in this key area, although he agreed that at a time when millions of people live beyond the protection of law, beyond the reach of human rights defenders, new approaches may be needed.

Stone was determined to know the organization from the ground up. As an outsider, he is expected to bring a new vision to the foundations; as one of its former grant recipients, he is expected to know how the process works; and as a former Vera Institute for Justice chief executive, he has an affinity for the Justice Initiative. It was at Vera that his path first crossed Herb Sturz's. It may have been Sturz who taught him how to be tenaciously persuasive, a trait that stood him in good stead when pushing for lighter sentences for the convicted and changing the justice system in the United States so it would not penalize young black men for being young black men. He worked in Russia and Turkey and was the founding director of the Neighborhood Defender Service of Harlem.

He was sure that I would note that his main concern is that OSF maintain its human rights, justice, and good governance focus in all its activities. That will include "improving the justice system even for ordinary criminals." In a country that imprisons more of its citizens per capita than any other in the world, that will be a welcome change. In a speech he gave on November 7, 2014, he talked of "America's bloated prisons ... an appalling and expensive failure, the politics of fear overwhelming common sense and human decency." He sounded hopeful that the electorate was beginning to see "this sham for what it is" and reduce or eliminate sentences for minor crimes.

Stone has known Neier for more than ten years, but professes to have been surprised when Neier told him he was on his personal shortlist of only eight candidates for the job. I don't know why. He has a great pedigree for almost any organization — even if you have to fill the shoes of Aryeh Neier.

He has degrees from both Harvard and Cambridge as well as a justice degree from Yale. An expert on criminal justice, he was a professor at Harvard's John F. Kennedy School of Government before joining Open Society. Stone protests he is anything but elitist. He says that Open Society is here for those people most in need of enfranchisement, people enduring oppression of all kinds. "Open Society wants to help remove the obstacles that prevent their voices from being heard, prevent them from feeling their own power," he said in his first video for Open Society. That work has kept him "going for the past many years in Harlem, Sierra Leone, South Africa, Papua New Guinea, Ethiopia."

He is personally supportive of Baltimore's Open Society Institute. It aims to keep children in school, make drug addiction treatment accessible, and reduce the number of people caught up in the criminal justice system. It's a complicated set of programs kept functioning by Diana Morris, who is the head of Open Society Baltimore. Morris had seemed concerned about maintaining her funding when Soros prefers programs with an end or a completion date. She told me she didn't see her program in Baltimore as easily completed but as ongoing.

No doubt, Morris would have found Stone's interest in connecting poverty to justice a welcome notion and felt relieved to hear that US programs would see an increase in funding in response to the financial crisis and the failure of the economy. Yet in 2012, funding for US programs went down about $50 million to make room for new expenditures.

Stone told me they would also spend more in Europe, Central Asia, and Africa to alleviate problems caused by the financial crisis.

It's interesting to note that Stone prefers open concept offices with no walls between work stations. His own desk is out in the open, and even the meeting rooms in the new Fifty-Ninth Street premises have only glass walls.

Leon Botstein had predicted that if George Soros does not give away all his billions during his lifetime, his foundations will go through an inevitable institutionalization. "I believe that institution-building in a civil society is transformative. But George doesn't." Botstein believes it will become difficult for the organization to avoid becoming bureaucratic. "I wish," Botstein said, "that there had been a sunset moment, despite how good some of his people are."[2]

IN
EASTERN
EUROPE

SEVEN

The Hungarian Experiment

I t was after he had made his first $40 billion that George Soros decided he was interested in finding worthwhile ways to give it away. He didn't need any more money for himself and his family; in fact, he didn't even need the $40 billion that he had already earned. He began attending Wednesday meetings of Helsinki Watch (later to become Human Rights Watch) to determine the best way to spend his fortune in the interests of building open societies — the concept he had been contemplating since his years at the London School of Economics. He listened a lot and went on a couple of "fact-finding missions" to South America. His first fledgling effort on his own was in South Africa and resulted in a substantial donation to open up Cape Town University to eighty black students. A year later, he discovered that the university had not done what it had agreed to do, and he discontinued the funding.

He helped a number of individuals behind the Iron Curtain with small donations, but his first foundation was set up in Hungary in 1984 under the aegis of the Hungarian Academy of Sciences, at a time when Janos Kadar's Communist government was still in control. He has usually said that his decision had nothing to do with his having been born there. As a Jewish child, he was an outsider in a society that had welcomed the

Nazis. He felt no kinship either to the place or to its people. He chose Miklos Vasarhelyi to help him realize his idea for a foundation that could co-exist with the Communists, while undermining their system.

Vasarhelyi had considerable publishing credentials, both as a journalist and as an editor. He had been the press representative of Imre Nagy's short-lived government of 1956, but unlike Nagy he was not executed following the unsuccessful Hungarian Revolution. A beneficiary of the 1960 general amnesty, he served only five years of jail time. By the 1980s, the economy was a shambles, and Hungary began to claw its way out of Communist fundamentalism. The regime counted on the forgetfulness of old enemies and announced, rather hopefully, that "he who is not against us is with us." During the years of what became known as "goulash Communism," it opened up investment opportunities for the West and allowed its citizens to develop a modest sense of entrepreneurship.

Vasarhelyi had been a fortunate choice. Both as a reform Communist and as a dissident, he enjoyed almost universal respect. His presence by Soros's side denoted integrity. It made dealing with functionaries easier, even when they were representatives of the ubiquitous state security service — the very men who had been responsible for incarcerating Vasarhelyi and his family in 1956. By 1985, as the Cold War began to dissipate, even members of the security service felt somewhat insecure and started planning for a future without all their current easy privileges.

For the first time in forty years, everyone was seeking compromises.

To convert dollars into Hungarian forints, Vasarhelyi came up with the idea of buying IBM photocopying machines for dollars and selling them to libraries and educational institutions for forints. In addition to endowing libraries with a genuine benefit, this fitted Soros's dream of helping create an "open society." Until the Soros-funded photocopying machines appeared, all photocopying equipment had belonged to the government. As the new copiers began to proliferate, the government lost control over information.

The forints could then be used for grants, and Vasarhelyi was particularly keen to fund youth programs. The new foundation handed out grants for innovative ideas, education, research, theatres, magazines, and arts venues. It subsidized publishing enterprises and computer literacy and provided copying equipment for universities. The foundation spent about $150 million in grants to individuals and organizations. Only a few years before, all this would have been deemed subversive. Now it was praiseworthy.

Soros believed that his ideas for an open society and his "critical mode of thinking" would encourage future leaders and give them a sense of how the rest of the world worked. There were scholarships for travel, for attending classes at foreign universities, and for books and journals that had not been available before.

In 1991, Soros also founded the Central European University in Budapest, one of a few privately funded universities in Europe.

"He doesn't, as a rule," Gara LaMarche told me, "believe in building institutions. It's the sort of thing Ford does. Not Soros." LaMarche ran Open Society's US interests under Aryeh Neier for several years. In that time, he learned a great deal about Soros, including the fact that he is not interested in construction projects, nor in sticking his name on buildings.

At first Soros rejected the idea of founding a university. He didn't think it was an effective way to influence a society. The best results, he said, are from inside a society, "infusing existing institutions with content" and allowing local individuals to spend money on causes they believe to be worthwhile. But he agreed with Vasarhelyi that there was a need in eastern Europe for a university that encouraged independent thought. Contrary to his usual habit of moving quickly once a decision had been made, he consulted with a formidable number of people he respected — Czech sociologist Jiri Musil, Hungarian historian Istvan Rev, statesmen such as Hungary's president, Arpad Goncz, and Czechoslovakia's president, Vaclav Havel — before determining the place and timing.

Initially, there were to have been three campuses or centres of learning: one in Warsaw, one in Prague, and one in Budapest. As it turned out, only one lasted. Prague stopped being accommodating when President Vaclav Klaus replaced Havel. Klaus, an otherwise businesslike statesman and an economist with some progressive ideas, had developed an intense dislike for Soros.

The Warsaw campus, which offered only sociology, struggled on until 2003, but failed to achieve either state support or the kind of credibility that would have inspired Soros.

That left Budapest. From the beginning it was a graduate university, cooperating with the best in the region and aiming to be the best. Janos Bojtar, one of the original faculty members, told me about the early years and spoke of his close friendship with Soros with obvious nostalgia. It was challenging to plan the curriculum and to figure out how to become accredited as a graduate school so that graduates could go on to good prospects.

"There had been such a lot of excitement in the air. But," he said looking out the window at the city, "many of the promises of those early years have died in the first decade of the twenty-first century." It is as if democratic thought had been merely an overlay. "Fascism remained underground, waiting for an opportunity to show itself." Bojtar was one of the old guard who helped create Fidesz, the centre-right party now ruling Hungary, but party members no longer talk to him and he no longer talks to them. Nor does he hear from Soros. I think he misses their lively exchanges and finds it hard to understand that people who had once been important to Soros no longer counted.

Istvan Teplan, another former Soros friend, one of the university's co-founders and its executive director from 1992 to 2007, believes that this institution may be Soros's greatest legacy: "The kids came to us with undergrad degrees from Zagreb, Warsaw, Bratislava; we trained them to Master's level. Many of them went on to Oxford and Cambridge and they did well." The focus remained the social sciences, the humanities, law, business, environmental studies, and public policy. The faculty, he said, was excellent in all subjects.

None of this came without the hiccups of fast growth and too much unquestioned funding, internal feuding, and occasional intrigue, although not more so than in most universities. Teplan was still bitter about former Rector Yehuda Elcana, under whose autocratic reign there were lavish dinners, even more lavish conferences, and some personal friends appointed to high positions.

Teplan is now director of the Hungarian National Institute for the

Environment. Soros never calls. He has a way of discarding friends, Teplan thought, once they are no longer useful.

Central European University's accreditation both by Hungary's Eotvos Lorand University and the State of New York in 1992, right after the inaugural class graduated, offered students the opportunity to transfer to other universities and to apply for scholarships and teaching positions elsewhere.

Today the university employs a diverse faculty from all over the world. Its extensive website proudly declares its "core mission": "The pursuit of truth wherever the inquiry may lead; a willingness to take risks and embrace new ideas; respect for the diversity of cultures and peoples; support for the integrity and dignity of individuals."

Its publishing arm, Central European University Press, has done a good job with a targeted list based on its expertise (e.g., Janos Kornai's *From Socialism to Capitalism* or Maria Todorova's *Balkan Family Structure*). The press's one overriding problem is a lack of effective distribution both in eastern Europe, where distributors are notoriously incompetent, and in the United States, where it remains a bit player.

The board chair is the peripatetic Leon Botstein. The university's president in 2014 was John Shattuck, another old friend of Soros. His appointment in 2009 was considered a sign that the university's single backer would not change his mind about continued funding. Soros's $250 million donation to the Central University Foundation confirmed his intention that the university should survive him. Every time I visited, the place was noisy and crowded with students and others having conversations in a myriad of languages. There were announcements of public lectures and scholarship opportunities. The halls were buzzing with loud discussions, cheery greetings, and rushing academics. Recently, the university has added two adjacent buildings, one of them a former palace, and expects to incorporate the nearby Open Society Institute.

Today the institute is a modest version of its former self. Kati Koncz runs it out of a plant-filled office with high windows, a few paintings, a black jacket that serves as a wall hanging, a couple of hand-woven carpets, a narrow desk, and wide chairs. The whole effect is that of a

home rather than of an office. Koncz is a remarkably attractive person
— cheerful, warm, and confident. She creates the impression of someone who has known you for a long time, but is just now catching up on
the news.

She had worked for other foundations including the Democracy
After Communism Foundation, where she learned how to write formal
requests for funding. One of those requests went to Soros, who offered a
little money if she agreed to work for him. A young idealist, she thought
working for Soros would help her make a positive difference in the world.

She went to Albania, Bulgaria, and Macedonia on his behalf. Then,
"George surprised me by telling me I was to go to Sarajevo. It was 1993.
I was in charge of an education support program when the war began."
She endured the shelling of Sarajevo and saw some of the children she
had supported die. Sarajevo changed her forever. It was the end of her
youthful optimistic belief that, after living under the controls of dictatorship, people would choose peace and democratic institutions. She saw
that they could just as easily choose ethnic nationalism and war.

Even in Hungary, things began to change. As the economy collapsed
under the Socialist government's incompetent management, people were
searching for someone to blame. The 2010 elections brought Fidesz to
power. According to arcane election rules, a 52 percent majority gave
Fidesz control of two-thirds of the House. They changed the constitution
several times, ended freedom of the press with the installation of their
own media board, accommodated the far-right Jobbik Party, and failed
to intervene against racist rhetoric in the media and in parliament. By
2013, when I met her, Koncz saw a "deep crisis of democracy."

Disappointingly, Fidesz was the party that she and the foundation
had supported. Many of its members had received Open Society grants,
studied abroad, learned about democratic institutions, the rule of law, the
coexistence of several points of view, and the idea that differences could be
discussed openly. Yet the party has dropped into the old well of xenophobia, populism, and a single way of thinking to the exclusion of all others.

"We spawned Fidesz," historian and Open Society archivist Istvan Rev
told me. Rev is a small man with a high forehead, unruly hair, grey eyes,
and expressive hands that fly about as he talks, and his careful, precise

delivery is a striking contrast to Koncz's warm, passionate voice. I first met him in 2009 after I read *Retroactive Justice,* his book about key moments in twentieth-century Hungarian history.

The name Fidesz, back in the late eighties, was an acronym for "young democrats," but as they aged, the "young" was forgotten — only the name stayed. Later, it seems, the democracy they had so enthusiastically espoused was also set aside. By the end of 2013, Fidesz was one of the least democratically inclined governing parties in the European Union. Prime Minister Viktor Orban is an Open Society graduate. Yet his party was criticized by the European Union, the United States Senate, and most Western media for restricting the press, encouraging a nationalistic shift to the right, and allowing a concomitant creeping anti-Semitism that has given the Jewish community reason to fear. The government's attitude to its Roma minority has been even more disturbing.

I asked Koncz whether there is still a point in having the foundation continue in Hungary.

"Our being here, staying visible, is of immense importance," she said. At a time when extremists are gaining ground, when Jobbik, the openly fascist party with about 20 percent of the popular vote, can spout its messages of racist hate, it is important for Open Society to remain visible.

"I live on Wallenberg Street [named after Raoul Wallenberg, the Swedish diplomat famous for rescuing Jews during the Holocaust]. At 11 a.m. last week, on my way to work, I was threatened by a group of black-clad youths shouting 'Heil Hitler.' They know who I am."

This is a time to be brave again.

Using Soros's definition, Hungary is a flop as an open society. The media are not free and pluralistic, but are controlled by the prime minister and his appointees; the judiciary is no longer independent; while the constitution protects minorities, the police do not, and the country lacks a safety net for the disadvantaged.[1]

The 2014 elections confirmed Fidesz's continued popular support. Hungarians seem to like the government's cashing billions of euros of EU funding while railing against the European Union, decking themselves in nationalist symbols, and accusing dissenters, including those who would prefer another political party, of treason.

Soros himself has come under sustained attack by the far-right media. He has been accused of operating a shadow government, and of having made his fortune from shady trade dealings, such as ammunition and landmine sales. When Human Rights Watch criticized the Hungarian government's legislation on violence against women, a minister blamed Soros. As Canadian author, journalist, and political commentator George Jonas put it, Soros could have become one of the most hated men in his country of birth for a lot less than $500 million.

The Open Society Board closed down the Open Society Foundation in Hungary in 2007. The decision was based on the belief that there were other, more endangered places, that with Hungary in the European Union, there would be other foundations and NGOs springing up to fill the void.

Istvan Rev is critical of Soros's decision to close down the foundation in Budapest: "Cultural support in Hungary was almost all Soros-funded. When it stopped, most had no idea how to support themselves." As Soros had feared, people had become dependent. That was precisely the opposite of the result he had wanted to achieve. Yet it had happened and now it was too late to undo it.

"Soros's idea had been that governments would support the programs after a while," Rev said. They have not done so. "As they would not, if Soros withdrew funding from the Baltimore project. It would just disappear." Presumably it would disappear together with all the good it may have done. "George never intended to become a humanitarian in the usual sense of that word ...We need to measure success in small increments, in the individual changes that we have been able to engender."

Rev told a story about two young men who came to Central European University, ostensibly as students, but their real agenda had been to kill an enemy from home. At the university, they got to know each other, went out for a drink, and the assassinations never happened. "Here, the Azeri can meet and listen to the Armenian, the Turk to the Kurd. It is an egalitarian university setting." There are other stories. "Here," Rev said, "Soros has succeeded in creating a place that may, indeed, lead to more open societies."

Given Soros's overall ambitions for not leaving a concrete monument in his wake, it would be ironic if Teplan was right and Soros's greatest single achievement, the real legacy project with staying power, would turn out to be the Central European University.

EIGHT

Eastern Promises

In 2012, US media commentator Bill Moyers said that George Soros had been the "most catalytic agent in helping to bring down the Communist governments behind the Iron Curtain." That may be a bit of an exaggeration, but he certainly was among the first to realize that the Soviet Union's grasp on its empire was loosening and that countries that had been ruled by the Kremlin since the Second World War were ready for independence. He understood that Solidarity in Poland was more than a local movement; that it had started a process that would spread throughout central Europe. He saw that Charter 77[1] in Czechoslovakia was an imminent threat to Soviet-style dictatorship, and that Kadar's "goulash Communism" was the last-ditch effort by the Hungarian government to breathe life into its dying rule. Soros had seen the signs. These countries craved change, and the Soviet Union was no longer able to assert its control. The empire was crumbling both on its periphery and from forces within. Internal divisions on policy and on new interpretations of the past were sending shock waves from Moscow to the provinces.

From the beginning of the 1980s, Soros had distributed funds to dissidents who were pushing for less rigid and unforgiving systems of government. There were packages of money for Solidarity strikers in Poland; signatories of Charter 77 in Czechoslovakia; Hungarian 56ers, many of them fresh out of jail; Romanian protesters; outspoken critics inside the Soviet Union, such as nuclear physicist Andrei Sakharov; Polish intellectuals; and Czech and Hungarian critics of the system who were still harassed by the infamous StB[2] and AVH[3]. In 1975 the Nobel Committee awarded the Nobel Peace Prize to Andrei Sakharov for his "fearless effort in the cause of peace among mankind." Soros served on the Sakharov Foundation's Advisory Board for a number of years.

There were years when the sole income for many central European intellectuals came from Soros, although most of them had no idea of the source. He paid for the printing of illegally distributed protest literature and backed concerts, art programs, conferences, foreign scholarships, academic libraries, international travel, and cultural initiatives that were not expressions of the prescribed dogma. The idea was that he would help people organize themselves, fund dissident voices, promote tolerance and democratic ideas, everything that was inimical to one-party dictatorships.

"Most unbearable for intellectuals was the lack of freedom of speech," wrote Wiktor Osiatynski in the preface to his book, *Human Rights and their Limits*, "The state's monopoly over the media, along with the strictest kind of censorship, made it difficult for ordinary citizens to learn the truth."

Osiatynski was one of the many students accepted for an Open Society fellowship. That gave him a chance to see the world. Since then, he has taught at US universities, lectured in Russia and Hungary on human rights, and is still on one of Soros's boards.

Istvan Teplan considers Soros's contribution in central Europe to be the single most powerful and lasting influence on the area since the Second World War. In his efforts to change how people here think, he supported Adam Michnik, who became the editor of Poland's most influential newspaper; Slovak film director Dusan Hanak; historian and politician Bronislaw Geremek; writer Gyorgy Konrad; playwright and politician Vaclav Havel; journalist Jan Urban; and philosopher Janos Kis —to mention just a few. These were the intellectuals who were listened to, even under the totalitarian system and even when they were jailed for their ideas. "To undermine the system, you have to do it through the mind," Teplan said. He had been among those intellectuals.

One of Soros's early beneficiaries, Kostek Gebert, still lives in a modest apartment in downtown Warsaw, but it's not nearly as modest as where he was in 1984 when Gebert first heard of George Soros from Aryeh Neier.

Gebert was one of the Polish intellectuals who backed Poland's Solidarity union's nationwide strike for the right to organize. The strike began in 1980 at the Gdansk shipyards and spread across the country. By 1981 the union had over one million members, enough people to scare Poland's Communist leadership into declaring "martial law." It was this handy law that empowered them to shoot demonstrators and imprison anyone considered a threat. This was not a regime that took pains to offer fair trials before slamming opponents into cramped jail cells.

Gebert was allowed to live under observation in his own home, which he describes as a "slum," although it was still much better than jail. He knew he was under observation, so he tended to look closely at anyone who appeared unannounced. When Aryeh Neier turned up at his door one day, Gebert said, "It never occurred to me that he was an important person," but there was something about the man that he liked, so he took the risk of inviting him in. At the time, Neier was with Helsinki Watch, the NGO engaged in monitoring the implementation of the Helsinki Accords.[4] It was soon to become Human Rights Watch.

"He offered me one of his cigarettes," Gebert remembered, telling the story of how Neier brought him a message from the Polish Underground wrapped up in a cigarette. The message gave Gebert hope that some urgently needed funds were available to help him organize fellow dissidents.

Neier had, personally, brought both cash and hope to Polish dissidents at a time when there seemed no hope for a change in Poland. Neier would join George Soros's Open Society Foundation in 1993.

When Gebert met Soros for the first time, he asked for a loan to start a radio station in Sofia. "We paid it back in a couple of years." Gebert, like several other early Soros associates, learned quickly how to become a small-time capitalist.

As president of the new Media Development Loans Fund, he invested in Latin America, Africa, and the Balkans. Between 1996 and mid-2012, the fund provided $115 million in affordable financing to a variety of independent media working in countries with a history of repression. The fund's first loan, as it turned out, was to the Slovak newspaper *Sme*, and it was paid back ahead of time. Thirty-eight million people, he told me, get their news today from clients of the Media Development Loans Fund. One Indonesian radio channel alone has eighteen million listeners and has become a "potent force for democracy." News outlets working with the fund saw their sales grow, despite the recession. Gebert is pleased to have been a part of that as is Stewart Paperin, president of the Open Society's Economic Development Fund, who provided the start-up investment for the fund and has seen fine returns.

Kostek is now a member of the team of experts on the European Council on Foreign Relations, a think tank that promotes discussions of a coherent and effective foreign policy for Europe. Launched in 2007, it was also originally funded by Open Society.

When we met in 2012, Soros was pleased to move into a discussion of his efforts to steer central Europe towards democracy during the late eighties. Those were, demonstrably, the most successful years of his foreign policy, a time when he saw himself emerging as a serious force in worldwide events. He was meeting with prime ministers, foreign ministers, leading dissidents, and church leaders, and was on hand to celebrate the demolition of the Berlin Wall — an international statesman, as he was characterized by newspapers at the time.

His idea, as he expressed it in an August 2009 essay for *Transitions Online*[5] was to provide an alternative to Communism's single vision. In Soros's view, there is never a single vision worth following. An open society allows for a multiplicity of visions and, even more threatening for dictatorships whether of the right or the left, disagreements. Failures and misunderstandings are part of the human condition.

"I approached the crisis in eastern Europe with a well-developed set of ideas about how societies work and how they change," Soros wrote in his *Underwriting Democracy*. He tried to become personally involved with ruling politicians where he saw a chance to influence their thinking. He tried to persuade General Wojciech Jaruzelski, Poland's last Communist president, that the only way out of the national crisis was a united front including both his supporters and his enemies. The country, with more than ten million striking workers, was ungovernable and economic sanctions were defeating every effort to appease the population. Jaruzelski's draconian martial law had been not only a display of unlimited power but also of his government's desperation. It was destined to fail.

Soros seemed pleased that Jaruzelski, whom I interviewed in 2008, remembered their meetings and mentioned Soros's influence in pulling together the Communist government figures and dissidents at a round-table meeting to discuss the future of Poland. By 1998, Soros had prepared the outlines of economic reform for Poland. He hired Harvard professor Jeffrey Sachs, a proponent of "shock therapy" and the "big bang" approach to economic reform (recently back from Bolivia, Brazil, and Argentina, where he claimed to have wrestled hyperinflation to the ground) to advise the fledgling Polish government on how to change from the central planning model of the Communist era to an efficient market economy. Sachs still thinks of those days in Warsaw as his major contribution to stability in the region.[6] No doubt he is pleased with the fact that during the years since 2008, Poland's economy has suffered the least of all the former Soviet republics.

Meanwhile, Soros became a superstar philanthropist.

In *Underwriting Democracy*, Soros writes about his 1989 visit to Estonia and Lithuania being "more like a state visit than a business call: I arrived everywhere by private plane with the crew of *60 Minutes* trailing me." He was beginning to enjoy the celebrity status that handing over money to cash-strapped eastern Europeans was bringing him. He now had direct access to the Czechs' Prince Karel Schwarzenberg who was in the first democratically elected parliament of the post-Communist Czechoslovakia, to Vaclav Havel the new president, and to his finance minister, Vaclav Klaus. He had similar access to the political leadership in Bulgaria, Romania, and Hungary. He had a "unique vantage point" from which not only to observe, but to direct how civil society evolved in eastern Europe. "Indeed, I began to act like a statesman," he said, and better still, he was able to outline his philosophy and new economic programs, bring in his own experts, and have every expectation that they would be taken seriously.

After his extraordinary success shorting the British pound in 1992, he declared he would devote even more of his money and energy to helping people unwillingly stuck behind the Iron Curtain since 1945.

He expanded his funding, set up local offices, and hired staff who distributed more money and more scholarships. By 1992 there were foundations in twenty-two countries. As the Soviet Union disintegrated, Open Society foundations blossomed in the Baltics, Yugoslavia, Georgia, and the stans. Open Society supported cultural endeavors in Albania and state-building in Macedonia. In Belarus, the Soros Foundation set about introducing "Internet culture," as an alternate way of reaching citizens.

In Poland today, Soros's Stefan Batory Foundation, named after a Hungarian nobleman who became the king of Poland and Hungary, still hands out scholarships to deserving individuals, institutions, and NGOs, although on a more bureaucratic basis than during its ad hoc beginnings. It has a website, a mission statement ("to build an open, democratic society — a society of people aware of their rights and responsibilities, who are actively involved in the life of their local community, country, and international society"), and a set of priorities that seems similar to those of other NGOs. Its budget in 2011 was $13 million, including $8 million from the Open Society Institute–Zug. It's a far cry from what it had been a few years ago, but there are now partners supporting the foundation's work.

Soros's success in the former Czechoslovakia is less obvious. The country split along ethnic lines into the Czech Republic and Slovakia. Czech president Vaclav Klaus had been hostile both to the idea of setting up a university in Prague and to Soros, personally. "We had a kind of behind-the-scenes battle," Soros said. "He refused even to appear on the same panel with me. I told him, 'I don't need you as an enemy.' He replied, 'What I resent is that you are trying to introduce socialism again.' That meeting helped me realize that even in former Communist countries, I had enemies both on the left and the right."

Perhaps one reason Klaus disliked Soros was his close relationship with Klaus's arch-rival, Vaclav Havel. "In the end, Havel, the dreamer, got the castle, Klaus got the country," Soros said. It's obvious he liked Havel, despite his view that Havel was an ineffectual politician.

Poland, the Czech Republic, Hungary, Slovakia, Slovenia, and the Baltic states joined the European Union in 2004; Romania and Bulgaria in 2007; and Croatia in 2012. Yet all is not well. In Hungary and the Czech Republic there have been an increasing number of racist demonstrations. The Open Society Fund in Prague promotes antidiscrimination and anticorruption in a largely unresponsive environment. Former dissident Jan Urban has spent the past several years exposing the corruption that pervades society — sometimes at the risk of his own life.

By the mid-nineties, Open Society's focus had shifted to issues on which the European Union was inactive or uninterested, such as the Roma. Ivan Krastev views the Soros organization's commitment to helping the Roma, although the effects may take a long time, as a singular success in Europe. Yet, sadly, the situation of the Roma is worse now than it was in 1989.

In Hungary, Soros told me, there is not a great deal to show for his efforts. The rise of nationalism, the so-called centre-right government's reforms to ensure it stays in power beyond its mandate, the end of press freedom, and the financial crisis all point in a direction antithetical to Soros's philosophy.

He was careful not to be openly critical of Hungary's populist Fidesz government. With his Central European University in Budapest, he has a lot invested in Hungary.

Serhiy Kudelia, a Ukrainian academic working in the United States, remembers the first time Soros-funded lecturers with Western degrees came to the Taras Shevchenko National University in Kyiv. It was exciting for students, but the local faculty remained hostile. They had been educated during the Soviet era and had no interest in changing how and what they taught. Kudelia saw it as "a clash of civilizations," but it may also have been fear that local academics could become irrelevant.

Soros helped Mikhail Gorbachev, who oversaw the disintegration of the Soviet Union. He tried to interest the United States government in a package of financial assistance for the Russians, akin to the Marshall Plan, that would have spared them the humiliation of their loss of empire, and might have saved them and the rest of the world from the rise of Putin. By 2014 it was difficult to discern signs of democracy in Russia.

In the lands farther east, there is even less to show for Soros's largesse. Deposed Georgian president Eduard Shevardnadze accused George Soros of engineering Georgia's "Rose Revolution," the public display of opposition that helped topple his regime. In 2003, Open Society funded a young Tbilisi activist to teach more than a thousand students how to stage a peaceful revolution and an anti-Shevardnadze television station that exposed corruption in government ministries. Twenty days of unrelenting street protests ultimately led to Shevardnadze's resignation. The tactics had been learned in Serbia, where popular demonstrations led to the resignation of Slobodan Milošević. In all, the foundations reputedly spent more than $40 million to unseat Shevardnadze.

Soros's friendship with opposition leader Mikheil Saakashvili, the man who succeeded Shevardnadze, no doubt influenced the decisions made by Open Society.[7] Alexander Lomala, formerly executive director of Open Society Georgia, went on to serve as a minister in the Saakashvili government.

When that relationship soured is not entirely clear. What is clear is that in 2008 Georgia marched into war with Russia over the disputed territories of Abkhazia and South Ossetia. When Saakashvili ordered his army into South Ossetia's capital, Tskhinvali, it was a foregone conclusion that Russia would counterattack. Saakashvili, who had studied at Columbia University, fallen in love with New York, and felt close to George Soros, may have assumed he would receive substantial encouragement from the West. If so, he was sorely disappointed. The presidents of Poland, the Baltic states, and some other east Europeans expressed their sympathies and verbal solidarity, but the United States offered only moral support. And Soros seemed to have changed sides. The larger-than-life, charismatic, passionate, temperamental Saakashvili, a man of great talents and appetites, and just as many foibles, was no longer his choice of Georgian leader.

In 2012, Soros flew to Tbilisi to personally congratulate Bidzina Ivanishvili. The new prime minister was also Georgia's richest man and leader of the rather optimistically named Georgian Dream Party.

According to *Transitions Online*, his personal fortune amounts to about half of the country's GDP. Georgia's electorate had turfed out Saakashvili and replaced him with an academic from the Georgian Dream party. Ivanishvili resigned before the 2013 elections, naming a long-time associate as his successor.

In Georgia, Open Society's stated aim is to "focus on human rights and development challenges," yet it finds nothing wrong with meddling with the country's internal affairs.

In 1997, after the arrest of the foundation's head, Soros closed his foundation in Minsk, Belarus. In 2012, President Alexander Lukashenko, Belarus's Communist dictator, once more demonstrated his brutal grip on power when the opposition failed to gain a single seat through parliamentary elections. The results were hardly surprising after the government's violent response to demonstrations demanding fair and free elections. Ballots were discarded, and the opposition was silenced. Those who have voiced disagreements have been jailed.

In 2012 Soros talked about his great disappointment in democratic reforms in Ukraine. The Orange Revolution of 2004 had been a failure. Back then, Viktor Yanukovych was still in power, democratically elected by an ostensibly knowledgeable electorate. The opposition was largely discredited or in jail, the judiciary was obviously not independent. The International Renaissance Foundation, the Ukrainian arm of the Soros Foundation, had contributed $1,653,222 to nongovernmental organizations implementing election-related projects.[8] It hadn't worked.

Still, Soros told me then, "there is Leonid Kuchma's[9] daughter, married to Viktor Pinchuk, one of the most successful oligarchs, a man with a media empire" in a place where freedom of the press was not even a dream twenty years ago, so there had been some progress. The Pinchuk Foundation, as it happens, supports causes that are dear to Soros's heart, and Soros believed a new generation of democrats might be rising from the graves of the old, unreformed Communist bureaucrats.

A lot had changed in Ukraine by the time of our February 2014 meeting. Soros was so ebullient about the Maidan revolution that had ousted Yanukovych's corrupt regime that he talked of Heisenberg's uncertainty principle applied to his own human uncertainty principle. "Subatomic elements can behave either as particles or as waves," he announced. "Same as humans ... they are either free-standing individuals or members of a movement or wave."

By March, Soros, who had been confident that the revolutionaries of the Maidan would succeed in establishing a democratic government, was beginning to see that ousting dictators doesn't always work. In a March 12, 2014, interview with Bloomberg News, Soros called the events in Ukraine "a wake-up call" for Europe. Russia had emerged as a rival to the European Union, and Putin had successfully outmanoeuvred the Europeans. European governments were squabbling among themselves, instead of meeting the challenge posed by Putin. As Soros saw it, Ukrainians had wanted democracy, the rule of law, responsible government, and all the other building blocks of the European Union — not unreasonable demands. Yet Europe had failed to respond. "I think Europe was totally unprepared for this crisis," Soros said. "But Putin had also miscalculated. He didn't realize that the Ukrainian public could rise up spontaneously."

By the summer of 2014 whatever hopes there had been for a peaceful, independent Ukraine had gone up in flames. Russia had already annexed Crimea and it was openly supporting separatists in the East with heavy armaments. Malaysian Airlines Flight 17 had been downed by Russia-supplied missiles. There were ongoing military clashes in Ukraine's eastern regions. All the International Renaissance Foundation could do was to "vigorously monitor events" and offer legal aid to activists and journalists.

Soros's prediction that Putin had nothing to fear from Barack Obama was proving itself on the ground. Soros's suggestion that the United States take punitive measures by opening its insufficient stockpile of oil to Europe, thus damaging Russia's economic power, was unlikely to deter Putin, whose threats of dumping US dollars may have had more potency that the US threat. Ukraine was settling in for a very tough winter without Russian gas. True to form, the European Union was not interested in Soros's ideas about how to help Ukraine. It voted on sanctions for Russia, but even those were not honoured by all its member states.

Petro Poroshenko, the new president,[10] was struggling to restore the devastated economy and tackle homegrown corruption, while engaging in military action against well-trained Russian troops. Soros's advice to the European Union was to concentrate on strengthening Ukraine, rather than punishing Russia. The EU is not in a position to oppose Putin's armies militarily. But "effective sanctions would discourage the inflow of funds" to Russia, Soros observed. "The Russian economy is fragile and vulnerable to smart sanctions."[11]

In his November 20, 2014, essay for *The New York Review of Books,* Soros warned that "Europe is facing a challenge from Russia to its very existence." He urged the West to provide an immediate cash injection of at least $20 billion to beleaguered Ukraine and suggested that the "European Union would save itself by saving Ukraine."

The Soros-funded International Crisis Group announced that Ukraine should stop trying to join NATO, thus attempting to appease the Russian bear.

In Uzbekistan, after spending $22 million on health care, education, culture, and democracy promotion, the Soros Institute was shut down by the government in 2004. Uzbekistan is the largest and richest state in Central Asia. Blessed with a wealth of oil and minerals, it suffers the fate of other countries with such wealth: uncontrolled corruption, an authoritarian regime, repression, and poverty.

Soros accused the Uzbek executive of running a government with the use of terror and torture and called unsuccessfully on the United States to suspend its relationship with the Uzbek government. But Uzbekistan's strategic importance to the United States during the war in Afghanistan outweighed the concern of US diplomats with human rights abuses. The United States traded its principles for expediency.

In neighbouring Kazakhstan, where the oil boom has proven the adage that mineral wealth is bad for human rights and worse for government accountability, Open Society has given $50 million to "like-minded NGOs".

In the face of government hostility towards civil rights groups, Open Society funded a range of NGOs in health care, education, and journalism in Tajikistan. In Pakistan, where politically and religiously motivated murder, anti-Western agitation, and a powerful military with an abysmal human rights record are accepted facts of everyday life, Open Society has tended to focus on education. Soros pledged an additional $5 million to help after the 2010 floods.

By the end of 2013, it was difficult not to feel disappointment in how democracy had failed to take root in the countries formerly behind the Iron Curtain. There are now dictators in Russia and Belarus. Romania is a mess. Ukraine is fighting for survival against a well-armed Russia. Belarus is a sump of corruption. The European Union itself has lost some of its former glow. The "shiny bauble," as Soros once called it, has been tarnished. It has allowed several of its members to sink into unmanageable debt. Germany's relentless demands for austerity have not worked. As the crisis worsened, Greece burned with righteous anger, Portugal and Spain begged for easier terms, and Italy tried to sell a reform package to its public. The euro was in danger of disappearing.

Ivan Krastev, political scientist, public intellectual, chairman of the Sofia-based Centre for Liberal Strategies, and founding member of the European Council on Foreign Relations, is another early Soros aficionado. He became involved with Open Society when it first invested in people and granted fellowships. For some of his colleagues, it was the most exciting time: the opening of a closed world. For Krastev, a Soros fellow at Oxford, it represented the freedom to think about the world in a broad context.

Today, Krastev, a tall, bushy-haired man with an attitude of absolute certainty, travels the world, lectures, and writes about the collapse of the Soviet Union, the Arab revolutions, the possible breakup of the European Union, the Russia-Georgia conflict, the problems of democracy, and Europe's legitimacy crisis, to name a few of his recent topics. His TED book, *In Mistrust We Trust*, has become a must-read for intellectual elites.

Krastev adds that one of Soros's most important and lasting contributions has been to "change how people see themselves in the world." They now relate to one another. Even in these times of a backlash against "liberal elitism," those who have accepted its ideas have proven to be survivors. Soros's convictions have permeated Europeans' way of thinking. According to Krastev, it is not his lasting effect on governments that one should consider, but his lasting effect on people. Nevertheless, the new entrants into the European Union have been repeatedly downgraded by Freedom House: their democratic systems have all deteriorated. Many have returned to old ways.

"The big difference," Soros said, "between investing in financial markets and investing in principles is that in the first case you do it to win. In the second, you do it to stand for the principles and sometimes you lose." Yet, he added, with a smile, "Sometimes the loss turns out to be a win."

NINE

The Failure in Russia

On November 7, 2003, just after midnight, a gang of masked Russians, wearing battle fatigues and wielding stun guns, stormed Open Society's offices in Moscow. They appeared to be dressed for quelling a riot, rather than for a potential confrontation with a few late-night office workers in downtown Moscow. They grabbed files, computers, and papers, crammed everything into their vans, and rushed off. Although it wasn't exactly surprising, the violence of the men was, nonetheless, unexpected.

Ekaterina Genieva, the executive chairman of Soros's Cultural Initiative in Russia, was devastated that the thugs had taken away all records of fifteen years of work.

It was the end of a dream that would have seen Russian society welcome democratic principles, such as an independent judiciary and a free press, a dream in whose pursuit Soros had spent about one billion dollars. During the 1980s, he had been impressed with Gorbachev's willingness to allow for the devolution of individual states and celebrated the breakup of the central controls that had kept the Soviet Union functioning. Soros was quick to set up foundations in each of the new republics with local advisory boards. While he admired Gorbachev, he noted that the Soviet leader was a good example of the "participant with imperfect understanding ... Specifically, he did not realize that dismantling the Stalinist system was not sufficient to bring about a free society." Had he known what was to follow, he might not have ended the old regime so quickly.

The same, incidentally, can also be said about Soros and his Russian foray. Predicting Gorbachev's failure should have been simple for a man of Soros's intelligence, but as a newly minted "statesman without a state," he was busy in too many countries at the same time.

He set up his first foundation in the Soviet Union in 1987, after he learned that Gorbachev had phoned the exiled Andrei Sakharov to suggest he should return to Moscow to pursue his "patriotic activities." That was the sign Soros needed that the Soviet Union was ready for change.

He started working on a scheme of financial and economic reform for the Soviet system. But his beloved Shatalin Plan[1] — an economic reform package devised by Soviet economists with some direction from Soros — failed to get Gorbachev's approval. Later Soros opposed the large-scale transfer of state property into private hands by the use of vouchers. These vouchers were distributed to the population in the expectation that citizens would become shareholders in formerly state-owned enterprises. Unfortunately, most Russians, who had grown up under Communism, had no experience with privatization, no idea of how the system would work, and no trust in their government's good will. Most were pleased to sell their vouchers for a fraction of what they were worth. The outcome was a number of large enterprises controlled by the few who knew how to game the system.

As the Soviet Union crumbled, Soros's Cultural Initiative invited applications for grants from across the country. The first forty recipients were varied enough not to raise suspicions: oral history projects, NGOs, a consumer group, a factory for manufacturing wheelchairs, an encyclopedia, a magazine ... Soros started to distribute emergency funds to scientists through the newly minted International Science Foundation for the former Soviet Union. The program offered $500 to any scientist who had published a minimum of three articles in reputable scientific journals.

In 1992 he donated $100 million to support the study of basic natural sciences. He funded the translation and publication of books by Western scientists and philosophers. He paid to have thirty-five Russian universities connected to the Internet. He was particularly keen to speed up the development of telecommunications. He said at the time that he believed that electronic communications were an integral part of developing open societies.

Soros had advocated for desperately needed funds from the West to bolster a vision for a new Russia with democratic overtones. He called for massive financial support along the lines of the postwar Marshall Plan that helped rebuild Germany.

Leonard Benardo, who was responsible for the Open Society offices in Moscow when they were raided, disagreed with the idea. "The state was in freefall. All the money would have been stolen," he told me. Despite Soros's vigorous efforts and his personal contributions, the West remained unmoved and during the summer of 1998 Russia's financial markets collapsed.

When Soros said in his book *Underwriting Democracy* that "what is needed now is to impose market discipline on the state enterprises," he misunderstood the Soviet system's utter incompetence. There were no functioning legal frameworks separate from the government. No independent judiciary. Regulations for breaking up government monopolies didn't exist. The financial systems had been imposed by central planning and crumbled without orders from above. The Soviet Union dissolved and Gorbachev left the stage, a defeated and discredited figure.

In 1990 he was succeeded by the charismatic but erratic Boris Yeltsin and the veritable storm of plunder that left Russia with only 50 percent of its wealth while the new oligarchs joined the West's rich and spoiled 1 percent.

Unfortunately, while Moscow had refused the full effects of Jeffrey Sachs's shock-therapy reform package, his ideas nevertheless permeated the financial reform process. He was there from December 1991 to December 1993 and advocated that the West advance around $30 billion to the Soviet Union. Later, Sachs claimed that it was not the reforms, but the efforts of powerful forces — endemic corruption and insider deals —

that destabilized the situation and led to the fiscal collapse. While Sachs takes credit for the rapid end of price controls, he claims his advice that a large-scale social safety net be established was ignored, as was his suggestion of massive international investment in Russia.

The International Monetary Fund, glaringly wrong in its own assessment, advised Russia to privatize quickly and without the necessary legal framework to make sure it benefitted the country. Russian banks were banks in name only. Their loans and investments had been dictated by the Communist Party. There was no "market" in the West's sense of the word, because all prices were set by the government.

As Joseph Stiglitz observed, the disaster could have occurred even without IMF's complicity in the form of its ill-fated $22 billion rescue package.

"The West," Benardo said, "did not understand the profound feelings of the Russians. Western advisors were clueless and condescending."

Both President Yeltsin and President Clinton expressed their appreciation of Soros's willingness to seize the moment and help some of the world's most accomplished scientists. In 1993 Yeltsin acknowledged Soros's financial investment in the foundation by exempting foundations from taxes and customs duties.[2]

In London Soros said that he was looking for a "megaproject" and it seemed he had found it in the crumbling remnants of the Soviet Union. A *Business Week* cover story said he was "most influential man between the Rhine and the Urals." In 1994, he joked in *The New Republic* that the "former Soviet Empire is now called the Soros empire,"[3] but in less than ten years the dream was dead.

In 1997, Soros pledged $500 million over three years to fund nursery schools, public health, and hospital services in the former Soviet Union.

In a 1998 letter to the *Financial Times,* Soros recommended the ruble should be devalued by 15 to 25 percent after the introduction of a "currency board." In an instance of the kind of unintended consequences that Soros the philosopher likes to ponder, he precipitated the crisis he had set out to prevent. His *Financial Times* article announcing that "the meltdown in Russian financial markets has reached a terminal phase" threw investors into the ditch and spurred inflation to 1992 levels.

And as the Russian currency plunged, Soros's own Quantum Fund lost $2 billion.

The IMF, prompted by the Clinton administration, provided the loans that kept Yeltsin in power for another term, just long enough to guarantee absolute corruption — the wedding of the Kremlin with the oligarchs. All of them became serially beholden to the equally corrupt government of Vladimir Putin, propped up by his former cronies in the security forces. A few years after the celebrations that greeted Yeltsin's accession to the position he so vitally desired, Russia's economy was in tatters, there were millions of unemployed, organized crime strutted openly in the streets, and there were shortages reminiscent of the old Communist days.

The man who took the most credit for the handover of power from Yeltsin to Putin was megabillionaire Boris Berezovsky, one of the favoured oligarchs. He escaped from the monster he had created and lived out the rest of his life in London. He had been a member of Yeltsin's inner circle and knew how to pull the levers of power. He had put his considerable resources behind television attacks on Putin's opponents. When he died in 2013, no one mourned his passing.

But the other man who could have taken the credit was George Soros. Leonard Benardo was there when Putin entered the stage. He saw how humiliating the anarchy, disorientation, and political fragmentation were for the Russians. Putin used the Russians' sense of hurt, disappointment, and despair and the failure of democracy to win their trust. He offered stability.

Putin had no sympathy for NGOs, particularly foreign-sponsored NGOs, and all that Soros stood for was anathema to the new, xenophobic Russian leader. Soros was an easy target: an American billionaire involving himself in Russian affairs even as the state was in freefall.

Post-Communist Russia is a failure in every measure that Open Society uses to assess democracy. Not much is left of the freedom of the press promoted by Soros and Western governments. It has become a dangerous place for journalists and for all those opposed to the regime. Journalist Dmitry Kholodov, who had been investigating corruption in the military, was killed by a briefcase bomb, human rights lawyer Stanislav Markelov and journalist Anastasia Baburova were gunned down, and Anna Politkovskaya and her friend Natalya Estemirova were both assassinated while revealing the Moscow-approved human rights abuses in Chechnya.

The murder of politician Galina Starovoytova demonstrated that being elected to mind the people's business was no protection from those who didn't want the state looking into theirs. Nor was there any pretense that corrupt bureaucrats and former secret service men could be accused of collusion. Lawyer Sergei Magnitsky, who had accused officials of fraud, ended up dead in his prison cell. And the roll call goes on. It is amazing that there are still some Russian journalists and investigators willing to put their lives at risk.

Not much is left of Human Rights Watch's efforts to name and shame Russia's ruling class of murderers. It is a regime with absolute impunity and not a scintilla of shame. In *The International Human Rights Movement*, Neier quotes Sergei Kovalev, former member of the Russian Federation's Congress of Deputies and later Chairman of the Presidential Human Rights Commission: "You wanted freedom? You thought that human rights were a universal concept ...? Just look what has become of Russia after communism ... And what can those of us who have not lost faith in the constructive power of democracy answer?" Kovalev had opposed Yeltsin's decision to bomb Grozny, and he vociferously opposed Putin's authoritarian rule.[4] Neier assumed that the only reason Kovalev has not been assassinated already was that, at over eighty, he was expected to die very soon.

In the late nineties, Soros was a vocal supporter of businessman Mikhail Khodorkovsky who, at the time, was the wealthiest man in Russia, and one of the richest in the world (ahead of Soros on the *Forbes* list). A former member of the Young Communist League, he had served as an advisor to Yeltsin's short-lived regime during the dying days of the USSR, snapped up state-owned enterprises when they were on offer, and ended up owning the most profitable of them all: the gigantic oil conglomerate Yukos. In 1998, he started a foundation called, with a nod to George Soros, "Open Russia." It funded, among other recipients, journalists in training and university courses. Soros admired the young oligarch for setting up a foundation, much like his own, whose aims included reshaping the way history is taught in Russia. He believed that the next generation would take a very different view of the world if they were not subjected to ideological bombardments rooted in old Soviet methods.

Kohodorkovsky was a Soros-style capitalist who said he favoured transparent transactions and board members who declared conflicts and didn't expect to be wildly rewarded for their activities. But he criticized Russian President Vladimir Putin and the system of cronyism, corruption, and willful blindness when Putin was dealing with the public interest.

Ekaterina Genieva, the last executive director of Open Society Russia, arranged the first meeting between the two billionaires. It was immediately obvious that Khodorkovsky liked Soros, and that the feeling was mutual.[5] Besides, Soros imagined that Khodorkovsky would provide him with an exit strategy, a joint foundation. As usual with all his charitable endeavours, Soros needed to see an end in sight to his Russian involvements.

Instead, Khodorkovsky, the only oligarch who had dared oppose the Kremlin's single-minded hold on power, was arrested, charged with fraud in 2003, and endured rigged trials. He was found guilty in 2005 and condemned to nine years in prison, a term that was extended in 2010 when he was judged guilty of embezzlement and money laundering and sentenced to an additional seven years. He spent most of his years of incarceration in Moscow's Matrosskaya Tishina prison, one of the oldest and least modernized facilities in Russia, where there is little light and no chance of outdoor exercise. In 2011 Khodorkovsky was moved to an old prison camp in the Siberian city of Krasnokamensk.

Open Russia Foundation has been shut down. Yukos was handed over to other oligarchs friendly to Putin.

Khodorkovsky appealed his sentences both inside Russia and in the European Court of Human Rights with equally dismal results. He was one of Amnesty International's prisoners of conscience and may have become the most trusted public figure in today's Russia.[6]

Soros noted that Russia had entered a phase of state capitalism — a form of government where the owners of capital recognize that they are wholly "dependent on the state."[7]

As Laura Silber, director of Public Affairs at Open Society, said at the time of the invasion of their offices, it had already become impossible to work in Russia. George Soros denounced Khodorkovsky's arrest and trials as a misuse of law, an outright "persecution." The invasion followed shortly after Mikhail Khodorkovsky's imprisonment.

In 2012 I asked Soros if he would he reopen his foundation in Russia if Khodorkhovsky was released. He said he would consider it, but when Khodorkhovsky was released on Putin's orders in the lead-up to the Sochi Olympic Games, Soros said he did not see this as a real release.

Soros has had to admit his ideas about Russia's reforms have failed. After his optimistic assumption that he could make a significant difference in Russia's post-Communist development, he was forced to recognize that his $1 billion had produced barely a ripple in Russia's march towards another Soviet-style dictatorship. Luckily Soros is fond of admitting mistakes and professing to learn from them.

Although Open Society Russia has closed, Ekaterina Genieva is a formidable woman who is still very much engaged with Russian society. As the absolute ruler of the Russia State Library for Foreign Books, she is a frequent guest speaker at cultural events throughout Russia and Europe. She is affiliated with various international organizations, including UNESCO. She is also a co-founder of the Russian Library Association and the recipient of numerous honours from a variety of literary orders. She has a wide, but somewhat suspicious face, with very sharp eyes, searching for what is behind the questions she is considering. What is wonderful about her face is her amazingly sunny, generous smile when she decides she doesn't need to be on her guard. Unfortunately, these moments are short-lived.

Genieva strongly disagreed that Soros's Russian foray was a waste. "George's legacy is embedded in the fabric of the country," she said. "Russia is becoming more open, more tolerant."

"The young generation is his real legacy," she said. Soros started the Pushkin Library program with $100 million, the Tula Internet Centre, the Pern Museum. There is a legacy of ideas that Genieva sees. "His special relationship with Russia, his respect for the people" never waned, she said. "As a Russian, I feel a moral obligation to acknowledge what George did here," she said.

"Without Soros," she said, "Prokhorov could not have happened. He may not have attracted a big vote, but he proved that people are not so afraid any longer." Mikhail Prokhorov, born in 1965, is another Russian billionaire, a former clothing reseller turned metals mogul,[8] more recently owner of the Brooklyn Nets basketball team, who was willing to risk taking on Vladimir Putin and his single-minded supporters during the 2012 elections campaign. He is the country's third richest man and, at six foot seven, its tallest billionaire by far. As part of his campaign, he suggested he would donate his billions to charity at home, if elected. Unlike the activists who organized the protests following Putin's rigged re-election to the position of president, Prokhorov could fund his own campaign. But the general assumption is that the Kremlin's usual band of thugs threatened him into abandoning his bid. The Kremlin hadn't allowed a select few to become billionaires at the state's expense only to see them step out of line. Since then, there have been no more rumours about Prokhorov in Russian politics. He has been partying and busy with his New York Nets.

In 2012 Putin announced that Russia had issued an international arrest warrant for Soros, claiming that Soros had used cross-collateralized Swedish and Danish currency derivatives to attack the Russian stock market. This may be a ridiculous charge that only a few people in the higher echelons of the financial world will understand, but what it signals to the rest of us is that Soros has become a pariah in the Russian state.

Genieva is sure Soros will be back. And the protesters themselves were a sign that Russians are waking up to the corruption and iron controls over their country. As Masha Gessen wrote in her book about Putin, *The Man Without a Face,* "something is in the air." During his December 2012 conversation with Sergei Guriev of the New Economic School in Moscow, Soros said: "For the last few months there has been an accelerating crackdown on civil society and on freedom of expression. This may unfortunately last, but not forever. Even in the darkest days of the Soviet Union the people's desire for freedom remained. It can never be extinguished." And he confirmed that he would continue to support Russian intellectuals. Perhaps Russians are not as "atomized," as Leonard Benardo feared.

During our 2014 interview, Soros said: "I am spending a lot of time on Russia, but the time for me to go back has not arrived and the fact that he [Putin] has released Khodorkovsky has not changed the situation ... Or it may have changed it but we don't know whether it's positive. The cause of freedom is not dead in Russia. It's evolving."

Perhaps the most significant monument to the Soros foundations' work here is the massive Russian Encyclopedia. At more than half a million words, 12,000 articles, and 11,000 illustrations, its online version has been operating since 2001. Its history had to be assembled from a range of wildly differing histories and negotiated with the schools that would be its most prolific users. My old friend Martin Grunwald, who had once run Facts on File's publishing program, is justifiably proud of the encyclopedia. It has been used in the schools and is browsed daily by thousands of children. But I was reluctant to ask what the encyclopedia said about Putin and democracy.

In September 2014, Khodorkovsky announced that he would be prepared to lead Russia, if called upon. Perhaps that was the sign Soros had anticipated when he said that the cause of freedom in Russia was evolving.

TEN

Meddling in the Balkans

Nestled inside a great valley along the Miljacka River, surrounded by the Dinaric Alps, Sarajevo has always been a place where different cultures — Serb, Turkish, Islamic, Catholic, Orthodox, and Jewish — have lived reasonably well together, despite the occasional clash. In her long, extraordinary travel book, *Black Lamb and Grey Falcon*, Rebecca West wrote of its charm, of feeling "like being gently embraced by a city," its exquisite Islamic architecture "in its restraint and amiability," its stolid, over-decorated Habsburg administrative buildings, the Serbian Orthodox cathedral, and the grand Catholic cathedral. But even in 1941 when West's book was published, the river ran red. West remarked on the phenomenon when she stood on the bridge over which the heir to the Habsburg throne, Archduke Franz Ferdinand, and his wife Sophie would have driven the morning of June 28, 1914, had they not been assassinated by a Bosnian named Gavrilo Princip. The assassination triggered the First World War.

Had West postponed her visit by a few months, she would have seen the city bombed, then occupied by the Germans and just a couple of years later by the Allies. Still, it survived all that, as well as its absorption into the newly created country of Yugoslavia, but it barely survived what became known as the Siege of Sarajevo. Shortly after Bosnia-Herzegovina declared independence in 1992, Bosnian Serb forces besieged the city. The siege lasted until 1995 and more than 10,000 people were killed, many while crossing streets, shopping at markets, or lining up for water or bread.

After the breakup of Yugoslavia in the early 1990s, George Soros set up foundations in each of the new states. The money earmarked for Bosnia may have saved more lives than the combined efforts of the world leaders and United Nations foundations that were engaged in the conflict, which turned into a mass murder or genocide. The United Nations exacerbated the suffering by declaring certain areas "safe" when they were not and UN forces had no authorization to fight. Yugoslavia was a humiliating lesson for the UN and a nightmare for its peacekeepers who had to stand by while men, women, and children were massacred. Both Srebrenica and Sarajevo were declared "safe," but neither city was.

Aryeh Neier, no stranger to atrocities during his work in South America, found the situation in Sarajevo "almost impossible to comprehend," and the reasons for the attack on the defenseless civilian population — a large number of whom were Serbs — were equally bizarre. They referred back to "supposed historical injustices during the centuries of Ottoman rule."[1]

Sarajevo, as it turned out, brought together some of those who remained with Soros's foundations for most of their working lives. It has become a memory of how a small number of people can make a real difference in a short time.

In 1993, when the city was isolated and surrounded, a Soros group went to Sarajevo to see how $50 million could be used most effectively to alleviate the suffering of the population under bombardment.

Kati Koncz, executive director of the Budapest's Open Society Institute, was there in 1993 when Neier arrived with writer-broadcaster William Shawcross. She also welcomed Neier's friend, swashbuckler Fred Cuny, who came armed with a $50 million donation from Soros, to establish the city's new water purification system. Cuny, a big, burly Texan engineer who stood six foot two and weighed 240 pounds, headed a Dallas aid agency, Intertect Relief and Reconstruction. He was loud, likeable, opinionated, confident, and fearless. His approach to humanitarian work tended to the unusually practical. He had worked in South America, Kurdistan, Biafra, Bangladesh, Cambodia, and Thailand. He had devised ways to deliver effective famine relief, build earthquake-proof houses, and distribute plastic sheeting for livestock. His trademark approach to all crises was that no problem was too great to handle.

Cuny arrived in Sarajevo courtesy of Neier and Lionel Rosenblatt, president of Refugees International. Both men had known him for a number of years and had faith in his abilities. Cuny decided the best way to help people was by restoring water, gas, and electricity. He brought in iron piping in Russian transport planes. Each plane would stay on the ground for less than seven minutes to avoid being hit by Serb machine guns. He managed to use most of the pipes to restore gas so people could heat their homes. "The freezing cold," as William Shawcross observed, "had been destroying lives, and morale was desperately low."

Cuny set up the water purification plant to supply fresh water to most of the city. Prior to Cuny's engineering efforts, people had to draw water from the wells with buckets, providing easy targets for Serb snipers on the surrounding hills.

Koncz was still trying to manage a $5 million educational fund when the shooting started. There were no lights or heat: "Classrooms were freezing cold. The kids sat in the dark, but everyone tried to carry on as if being shot at was part of a normal day."[2]

The most infamous killing spree occurred in February 1994 when a bomb was dropped into the city-centre marketplace, near the Catholic cathedral. The initial count of the dead was sixty-nine, but it grew as many of the wounded died. The Bosnian Serbs denied responsibility, but only someone very naïve could imagine that anyone other than those already in the habit of lobbing bombs into the city could have been responsible.

"Sarajevo changed the way I think about humanity," Koncz said. "Those days with the Serbs bombarding the city and no help from the outside world. George was one of the few who really helped."

The man who still haunts her memories, just as he haunts Neier's, is Fred Cuny, who was killed in Chechnya. Cuny had advocated setting up an international crisis group that could deal with catastrophic situations, such as the one in Sarajevo. The International Crisis Group was formed in 1995 with an initial annual budget of US$20 million. Its mandate was to work out strategies and detailed recommendations to avert or limit crises. Soros still sits on the executive committee.

Jan Urban, a leading figure in the Velvet Revolution that freed Czechoslovakia from Soviet rule, covered the war for the Soros-backed online newspaper *Transitions Online*. He was in Sarajevo during the Serbian bombardment and remains critical of the United Nations and NATO for their incompetent presence there during that period.

Laura Silber, now in charge of communications and public affairs for Open Society, first met Neier when she was covering the war in Yugoslavia for the *Financial Times*. She was a consultant on the BBC's documentary series *The Death of Yugoslavia* and coauthor of *Yugoslavia: Death of a Nation*. She received an Open Society Fellowship grant for the book, which sets out to prove that Yugoslavia did not die a preordained death caused by centuries of animosities in an incomprehensible part of the globe, but was systematically destroyed by a group of men seeking power. In particular, she studied the murderous methods of Slobodan Milošević and the ineffectual efforts of the European countries to stop the bloodshed. The United Nations proved unequal to the single task of preventing the murder of civilians.

It was in Yugoslavia that Silber met NATO commander General Rose and his opponent General Mladić. It was also in Yugoslavia that she saw the results of incompetent politics meeting an implacable force and the destruction of Srebrenica where seven to eight thousand men and boys were murdered by Serb forces. The experience may have been the decisive factor in Silber's change of profession.

The war in Bosnia officially ended in 1995 with the signing of the General Framework for Peace in Bosnia-Herzegovina at Wright-Patterson Air Force Base in Dayton, Ohio. What is usually referred to as the Dayton Accord was signed by Richard Holbrooke on behalf of the United States. Holbrooke, to his credit, refused to offer amnesty to war criminals.

The deal cost the United States and Europe about $45 billion in aid. In Soros's opinion, the aid was guided by "dogmatic market fundamentalism." He believes that this is exactly the kind of support that is destined to fail both the donors and the recipients. It is driven by outsiders with no knowledge or understanding of local conditions and no effect on local policies, whereas the "Open Society Foundations seek to shape public policies that assure fairness in political, legal, and economic terms."

Twenty years after the end of the war, Bosnia-Herzegovina is one of Europe's poorest countries. The ethnic divisions that underlay the wars of the nineties are still evident in Sarajevo. As 2014 limped out of the city, it was good to consider the anniversary of the First World War and whether it started by accident or whether the causes were evident for years, but no one wished to notice.

IN 1999 YUGOSLAVIA endured eleven weeks of NATO bombing that resulted in about five hundred civilian deaths. Today, members of the former Yugoslavia remain ethnically divided, mostly impoverished, and behind their neighbours in the rush to join the European Union. Ivan Vejvoda, now director of programs for the German Marshall Fund of the United States, worked for Open Society during the most turbulent period in Yugoslavia's modern history. At that time, there was still a Yugoslavia, although it had shrunk to only two of its member states: Serbia and Montenegro. Although he was still teaching at Smith College, Vejvoda became executive director of the Fund for an Open Society in Belgrade in 1998 and stayed for four years. He was attracted to Open Society because he noticed the foundation always chose leaders from among local people who had an understanding of the place where they worked.

"With the country under sanctions at the time, our work with civil society was vital," he said.[3] He believed that maintaining the arts, sciences, universities, news, and cultural media were an important part of resisting the rule of Milošević, then president of the Federal Republic of Yugoslavia as well as of Serbia. Milošević censored the press, restricted free speech, strengthened the army, and imprisoned opponents. The fund brought in printing presses so publishers could continue to print books, journals, and magazines and funded translations and independent radio. They started with a budget of $15 million, but it soon grew to about $300 million.

Milošević's intention to create a greater Serbia, free of non-Serbs, in what he considered to be the Serbs' rightful territory was apparent as early as 1987. The expulsions of Bosniaks began with the burning of their homes and gang rapes of the women, and ended with mass graves where unarmed young men and boys were dumped.

Through 1998 and midway through 1999, the Yugoslav army battled with the Kosovo Liberation Army, backed by NATO, for control of Kosovo, which was then a province of Yugoslavia. Kosovar Serbs fought to gain control of territories by expelling the non-Serb population. Expulsion turned, at some point during that year, to murder. By 2000 the bodies of more than 3,000 Kosovo Albanian victims had been recovered.

Open Society in Serbia supported Kosovo's Albanian minority and helped Macedonia feed and house Kosovo Albanians forced to leave their homes. The Kosovo Foundation advocated for Kosovo within the European Union and helped secure billions of dollars in development assistance. Soros, of course, was accused by both the Serbs and the Albanians of meddling in Kosovo's affairs. Soros didn't make any friends in Belgrade by lobbying for Kosovo's independence. The Kosovar government alleged that Soros's interventions were unwelcome, while the US right-wing press accused Soros of planning to plunder Kosovo's wealth. Kosovo has the richest natural resources in the Balkans: gold, silver, lead, zinc, cadmium, bauxite, copper, and coal.

"When NATO began its seventy-eight days of bombing, Sonya Licht and I decided to stay in Belgrade," Vejvoda said, "even as the rest of the city began to evacuate. We thought if we left now, we would not be able to look ourselves in the face." Sonya Licht,[4] a sociologist, had been a leader in the Yugoslav dissident movement and became executive director of Open Society in 1991. Vejvoda followed her. They are both Serbian.

Briefly, he worked for Serbian Prime Minister Zoran Djindjić, a founder of the Democratic Party in opposition to Slobodan Milošević, as senior advisor on foreign policy and European integration. It was Djindjić who handed Milošević over to The Hague's criminal tribunal for prosecution. He was assassinated in 2003 by a former special forces operative.

Vejvoda is a strong believer in Serbia's future as a member of the European Union, and thinks his views are shared by the population, despite the NATO bombing and the 2008 worldwide recession. Even after the 2013–14 floods, Serbia is doing better economically than its former partners in Yugoslavia. The government is stable and European accession is on the way. Open Society Foundation Serbia supports European integration and the usual Open Society constants of good governance, justice, social inclusion, and human rights. It has been particularly active in its efforts with the European Roma. Zeljko Jovanovic, charged with improving the situation of the Roma, is from Serbia.

The International Criminal Tribunal for the Former Yugoslavia was established by the United Nations Security Council in 1993.[5] The court classified the Srebrenica killings as genocide, but the debate over the nomenclature continues in both Serbia and Bosnia. It has indicted 161 former Yugoslavs, including former Bosnian Serb General Ratko Mladić and former Bosnian Serb leader Radovan Karadžić for their roles in the shelling of Sarajevo. David Scheffer, who served as the first US ambassador for war crimes, wrote about the difficulties of bringing to justice those who were responsible for the massacres.[6] The US military, the Pentagon, and the CIA under the Clinton Administration all refused to turn over intelligence and satellite photos that proved the allegations against the perpetrators. That, he wrote, explained why it took more than ten years to bring Karadžić and Mladić to justice.[7]

The tribunal and its observers endured more than 7,500 trial days and viewed 1.6 million pages of transcripts as of May 2013.[8] Slobodan Milošević died in 2004, part way through his trial. As prosecutors were preparing the indictment against former Croatian strongman Franjo Tudjman, he also obliged his enemies and disappointed the tribunal by dying at home.

Critics of the International Criminal Tribunal for the Former Yugoslavia — some people call it "Soros's Court" — charge that it has encouraged people in the Balkans to live in the past, rather than deal with it and move on to reconciliation. They charge that it has not helped people to work out ways of living together, although that could change when the European Union admits them all as members. Many of the court's proceedings have been unnecessarily complicated and inconsistent. Too many accused were acquitted because of a lack of satisfactory evidence.

As Neier saw it, while the proceedings have been slow and often unsatisfactory, they had a positive effect on local judiciaries and civil society. The survivors desperately need a measure of justice, even if it takes a long time and brings little satisfaction when it does arrive.

Open Society's Ivan Krastev's conclusion is that the tribunal, like the International Criminal Court, is not trusted by former Yugoslavs. "Human rights people, like Neier, do not believe in politics. They believe in virtue." That is impossible to come by in situations where people are involved. Virtue has no place in politics.

In his article "Never Again: Judgments on a Decade of Bestiality," Mirko Klarin, editor of SENSE News Agency,[9] said that the tribunal's "real legacy will depend on how the courts of these countries continue their work in the years and decades to come ... Civil society ... faces an uphill battle against denial in their effort to promote historical reflection and confront the past."

Open Society has established law centres in Bosnia and Serbia.

Croatia shut down its Open Society Institute in 1997, when President Franjo Tudjman accused the foundation of supporting his opponents. It was a charge Soros did not bother to deny. Opposing the thuggish Tudjman would have been an obvious thing to do for a guy who believes in open societies. Croatia upped the ante by convicting two Open Society employees of tax fraud. Although there were still scholarships available to new applicants, the Open Society Institute closed shop in Croatia in 2006.

The foundation reopened in 2011 under new leadership and with brave new words of support for a country beset with economic problems and threats from inside and outside as the European Union struggles with its own demons. Nevertheless, Croatia opted to join the European Union on July 1, 2013, amid fears by Germany and Austria that cheap Croatian labour will flood their countries.

In its issue of July 26, 2014, *The Economist* rated Croatia "a mighty mess" and Europe's latest "basket case." Joining the European Union has not brought new prosperity, nor the required impetus to reforms.

Soros's role in Macedonia, like his support for Jeffrey Sachs's African dream, remains a puzzle for many Open Society insiders. The tiny landlocked country with a population of only two million and an ongoing battle with Greece over its name, has enjoyed a great deal of Soros funding ever since his first visit there in 1992. Ivan Krastev says Soros is always attracted to those places no one else cares for. Macedonia had no one on its side. In his 2002 biography of Soros, Michael Kaufman tells the story of Soros impulsively awarding a $25 million loan to the country's president, Kiro Gligorov, for trying to preserve Macedonia's multi-ethnic character. Of course, the former Communist apparatchik did no such thing, and as this became obvious, even Soros became critical. But in 2013, Macedonia still received more than $6 million in Open Society funding.

Krastev used to be merely Bulgarian, an early beneficiary of a Soros scholarship, but he is now a man of the world. In addition to his position on Open Society's global board, he is also board chair of the Open Society Initiative for Europe with 2013 expenditures of $19 million. The director of the Initiative for Europe is Jordi Vaquer, whose first experience with Soros's foundations was in the former Soviet states and in the Balkans. The Balkan countries, Krastev said, are looking to move on from the past, not dwell on it.

Krastev's latest book is *In Mistrust We Trust: Can Democracy Survive When We Don't Trust Our Leaders?* The question is certainly an interesting one to ponder at a time of crisis in Europe.

ELEVEN

The Struggles of the Roma

The Charter of Fundamental Rights of the European Union sets out in mind-boggling bureaucratese guarantees of dignity, freedoms, equality, justice, solidarity, and rights that all citizens of the union should expect of their countries and fellow citizens. It boasts of the union's spiritual and moral heritage and its commitment to the principles of democracy. The charter was enthusiastically signed by all the presidents of the European Parliament at the European Council meeting in Nice on December 7, 2000.

There is no mention in this laudable document that these rights do not apply to the ten to twelve million Roma who live in Europe. It's impossible to be definitive about how many Roma there are because so many do not admit to being Roma or "gypsy," as they have been called in a slew of languages in eastern and central Europe. Given the overt prejudice they endure, that is hardly surprising. The European Union's Decade of Roma Inclusion was launched in 2005. Each of the twelve nations that signed on to the decade, all with significant Roma minorities, undertook to close the gap between the Roma and non-Roma populations in education, housing, and health and to alter the cycle of poverty and exclusion that the Roma had experienced in previous decades. These nations pledged to devote resources to combating prejudice. The United States, Norway, and Slovenia have observer status. The money was contributed by a range of countries and organizations interested in human rights, chief among them the Open Society Foundations.

Eight years after the charter of rights was signed, I travelled through Europe looking for signs of the Decade of Roma Inclusion and found very few. It was hard to think of dignity when confronted by armies of rats in the ninth district of Kosice, Slovakia, where nine or ten Roma families live in dank, cold, and dark rooms (no electricity, no heating, broken windows) in Soviet-era concrete apartment blocks. Children play among the rats and mountains of garbage. In Ostrovany, Slovakia, the non-Roma part of the village built a two-metre high concrete wall to separate it from its Roma neighbours.

The majority of Roma children in the Czech Republic and in Hungary are still segregated into separate classes for the mentally challenged. They face the same problem in Croatia, a new member of the European Union. The European Court of Human Rights condemned the practice several years ago, but nothing has changed.

Meanwhile, the Czech Republic has seen growing support for the extremist Workers' Social Justice Party, which has held marches in towns where the Roma live. The party organized petitions in support of a man responsible for murdering a Roma boy with a bow and arrow. In Prague, three youths were arrested for the brutal killing of a Roma woman.

One visit to Tiszabura, Hungary, would convince even the most oblivious that the filth, misery, cold, and hunger endured by the Roma cannot be what the European Union meant by "benefits."

In Bulgaria, Ataka (which means "Attack"), the far-right party with openly anti-Roma sentiments, holds twenty-one seats in parliament. They march wearing black shirts and carrying banners with the slogan, "I do not want to live in a gypsy country." Hungary's Garda wear similar uniforms and carry similar banners.

In 2010 France offered significant bribes (€300 each) for Roma to return to the east. The minister of the interior declared that the Roma cannot coexist with other Europeans. Meanwhile, Italy has ignored vicious attacks on Roma camps while the police packed Roma off to other EU countries.

In a September 2010 speech directed at European policy-makers, Soros tried to steer the conversation in a positive direction. "The greatest divide between the Roma and majority populations is not one of culture or lifestyle but of poverty and inequality ... Roma share the same aspirations as the majority populations: a home with adequate services, a decent education for their children, and jobs that enable them to provide for their families. It is because they face appalling discrimination and deprivation at home that they continue to migrate across Europe."[1]

Worse even than the physical hardships is the pervasive fear. Racist extremists threaten Roma children and throw bricks at Roma homes throughout the Eurozone as local police stand by.

"The problems of the Roma are deteriorating with the economic situation. And the majority of the public is releasing its anger and frustration at its own economic situation by attacking the Roma," Soros told the EU Observer in November 2010. It was the same message he had taken to the European Union. The Eurozone crisis that began in 2008 has had a particularly dangerous effect, with nationalist fervour on the rise and extremist parties throughout the region seeing a sharp increase in support. Vicious attacks on the Roma have become commonplace.

Hungary's ultra-right Jobbik Party has blamed the Roma for all petty crime, and the ruling party, Fidesz, has established workfare for the Roma in closed camps reminiscent of the Nazi labour camps of the 1940s. Workfare often consists of meaningless work, such as picking up and replacing firewood.[2] And the Hungarian police union has signed a cooperation agreement with Jobbik. In 2012 an off-duty Slovak police officer killed three Roma at random. In Romania two unarmed Roma men were shot and killed by the police in early 2012. Is it any wonder that Roma do not go to the police to complain about harassment?

Persecution is not new for the Roma. They were forcibly sterilized in Czechoslovakia and Slovakia between 1971 and 1991 as a government-sponsored effort to reduce the Roma population. The procedures were performed on women without their knowledge during Cesarean sections and abortions. The Czech ombudsman estimated that more than 90,000 Roma women had been sterilized in this way. Unfortunately, researchers for the Roma Rights Centre have reported that there are still new cases coming to its attention.

Roma slavery in Moldavia and Wallachia (present-day Moldova and Romania) persisted for about five hundred years and still continued long after it was abolished in 1850.

During the Second World War, the Nazi regime and its collaborators transported Roma to forced labour camps and annihilation sites. While thousands were shot at the edge of villages, many others were deported to mass-killing sites, gassed, beaten, or starved to death. In Auschwitz-Birkenau alone, about 250,000 Roma were killed. Nobody kept count of the dead.

During the post-war Communist dictatorships in the Eastern bloc countries, the Roma's traditional way of life, which was mainly agricultural, was ended. They were forced from their villages and moved into Soviet-style concrete apartment blocks so they could be closer to the factories where they worked. They remained uneducated and unskilled. With the arrival of capitalism, their factory jobs ended, but nothing replaced them. Before the 1990s about 80 percent of the Roma in eastern Europe were employed; afterwards 80 percent became unemployed. Various governments moved them into Roma areas where no one worked, and everyone starved.

This is the grim challenge Soros chose for the Open Society Foundations. Their programs include workshops for the Roma on advocacy and health and education in history, media, communications, and civil and human rights.

At the Second Roma Summit, held in April 2010, Soros said that the "key is to educate a new generation of Roma who succeed in society but do not seek to melt into the general population and retain their identity as Roma. Educated, successfully integrated Roma will shatter the prevailing negative stereotypes."[3] In 2009 the Open Society Foundation directly assisted 30,000 Roma children and 800 university students. "Europe cannot afford another lost generation of Roma," Soros said. He spoke of an urgent need to make room for the Roma in the labour force. As Europe's population is greying, the Roma present an opportunity for new, educated, tax-paying workers. As of the end of 2012 Open Society had spent about $200 million on Roma education alone.

In an effort to break down Roma stereotypes, Open Society has provided financial assistance to more than one thousand Roma medical students. A 2014 video posted by Open Society shows a group of young Roma doctors on a train travelling through Romania, joking about their lack of musical talent[4] and offering medical care to the needy.

While the effort is exemplary, according to Aladar Horvath, head of the Roma Civil Rights Movement in Hungary, it serves more to create a Roma elite than to influence how the Roma are viewed in society or to help the majority who struggle for minimal survival in countries that accept violent attacks on them as normal. Even with the European Union's substantial funds, he sees little appetite for change. Millions of dollars have been soaked up by conferences and studies, he said. Some Roma leaders have even accused the small Roma elite ensconced in NGOs of spending the aid money on themselves.[5]

A burly man with an unruly grey beard, Horvath was a member of the Hungarian parliament during the nineties. But he remained cynical, both about the intent behind putting him there and about his own achievements as a parliamentarian. He told me while we were travelling in his decrepit car towards Tatarszentgyorgy, a village infamous for the murders of a young Roma boy and his father, that the job was merely a "pacifier." It had the patina of power without the means to accomplish anything. He had been relieved when it ended.

Horvath, who has received several Open Society grants in the past, is no longer on the Budapest centre's recipients list. "He lacks servility," according to one of his associates, "plus the ability to fill out the necessary forms to account for funds, though it's absolutely obvious he has not, personally, taken any of the money."

"He is the kind of man Open Society's Roma Centre needs to listen to," Laszlo Szoke argued. "[He is] someone who has pride and a vision for the future of his community. The trouble with Open Society here is their attitude that they always know best."[6] Szoke is a most unlikely Roma activist. He is a blond Jewish American with a sunny disposition and a conviction that he can do some good.

Bernard Rorke, who teaches a Roma Rights course at Central European University, used to be director of Open Society's Roma Participation Program. Its policy, he said, was direct support of Roma and Roma NGOs. "Our idea was that only Roma could emancipate themselves. We wanted the centre to be Roma-staffed and Roma-led." In these areas, they have succeeded. Nor does George Soros seem concerned that his funds have created a Roma elite.[7] The elite are the Roma's future leaders, in his view. Creating a new generation of political and economic leaders has always been one of Open Society's ambitions.

The man responsible for all Roma programs across the region is Zeljko Jovanovic, a Serbian Roma who joined Open Society in 2006. He is young and stylish in a tight dark suit and open-necked white shirt. He barely stops for breath while he answers two cell phones, giving instructions on an upcoming event and trying to schedule a meeting somewhere in northeast Hungary. He says his work includes making society care. "We now have supporters in the European community and in national governments. But the Roma need political power, their own strategies to make governments act on their commitments."[8]

In a recent speech in Washington, Jovanovic sounded a lot less positive: "We believed for many years that democracy would work for Roma in Europe. It hasn't …The Roma have been and are still scapegoated in countries all across Europe … Perhaps worst of all in Hungary where attacks on Roma villages, firebombing of Roma homes, and killing of Roma picked at random by right-wing extremists have occurred."

In March 2011, Amnesty International wrote to Hungary's prime minister protesting the lack of official intervention on behalf of the Roma in Gyongyospata where right-wing vigilantes invaded the town and threatened the Roma population.

Canada was, until recently, at the receiving end of the Czech Republic's and Hungary's Roma refugees. To stem the tide, the Canadian government reintroduced visa requirements for Czechs in 2010. Then, at the end of 2012, the minister of immigration decided that Hungary was a "safe country." Since Canada doesn't take refugees from safe countries, it would no longer be accepting Roma refugees from Hungary. It wasn't an unpopular decision. Most North Americans, including Canadians, first learn of the Roma when they are warned about pickpockets and purse snatchers in countries they like to visit in Europe, where young Roma have perfected the art of relieving tourists of their valuables. In its September 2011 issue, *Paris Match* ran a long article, complete with photographs, of a band of young female Roma thieves thriving on the tourist trade.

But is Hungary safe for the Roma? The Harvard School of Public Health issued its own warnings in February 2014. "Accelerating Patterns of Anti-Roma Violence in Hungary" reports on racist public statements of hate by mainstream parties and the increasingly virulent rhetoric by the Jobbik Party and its militant members. It is hard to read this with the Canadian government's "safe country" designation in mind.

In 2014 in Greece, there was the case of the blond Roma child in the home of dark-haired Roma parents, who were accused of kidnapping. The story went viral. Its resolution — the impoverished birth mother explaining that the couple had informally adopted her child and were raising it — did not. Other cases and accusations — all without foundation — surfaced in Ireland and Italy. The stereotype of the "evil other" persists in the popular imagination.

The Council of Europe's own assessment, as expressed in yet another report confirming what everyone already knew, is that not much has changed since the Decade of Roma Inclusion began.[9] There have been many studies, a veritable mountain of documents, but not a lot of positive change. About the only happy note in this grim publication is that more Roma are taking advantage of educational opportunities, but that is meagre solace for the millions afflicted by violence and lack of even the most basic human comforts.

Despite Bernard Rorke's heartfelt contention that a significant part of Soros's legacy in Europe is his commitment to the Roma, it is hard to see the results of Open Society's interventions. It is difficult to verify his claim that OS has created a "heightened level of awareness worldwide, and a sense of urgency" in Europe. In a September 2012 *Open Democracy* article, even Rorke sounded dispirited: "It is clear that the populist political imperative to get tough on immigration in general, and Roma immigrants in particular, takes precedence over any deliberations about what might make for a sustainable and humane policy on managing the migration of the European Union's most disenfranchised and impoverished citizens."

In Sudetic's *The Philanthropy of George Soros*, Soros says: "Of all the activities in which my foundations are engaged, addressing the problems facing the Roma is the one with which I have been most personally involved … The character of our programs reflects my personal influence: they are diffuse, diversified, and well funded." Yet, despite that, they have failed to make a significant difference.

Perhaps in 2017, at the end of the Decade of the Roma, there will be a new assessment.

SPREADING
ACROSS
THE WORLD

TWELVE

African Expeditions

Soros started his philanthropic activities in South Africa in 1979, long before he declared his intention to change the world. He thought he would offer scholarships for black students to attend Capetown University. The university, however, used the funds for the few "coloured" students already enrolled, rather than admitting new ones. After that debacle, Soros stayed out of South Africa until the end of apartheid.

Herb Sturz, who had worked on New York City's Queens West Project, Vera, and The Bowery, came to South Africa in 1994 when Nelson Mandela was president, to build houses for people who couldn't afford to have homes. It was a huge success.

It was Neier who first mentioned to Sturz the housing crisis in the new South Africa. George Soros committed $5 million immediately and a further $50 million in guarantees to assuage the skittish banks' fears. Sturz, the legendary New York troubleshooter, still talks of the speed of the development and its success in attracting ordinary South Africans. By 2007 there were 200,000 homes, community centres, and even gated communities for the black middle class.[1] Sturz's village remains one of Soros's most successful initiatives.

The Open Society Foundation was established in South Africa in 1993.

Today, it is still handing out money to people and causes that suit its mandate with funding in 2013 standing at $7 million. The foundation's stated aims include "democracy, a market economy, a strong civil society, respect for minorities and tolerance for diverse opinions," even as nepotism, corruption, and violent crime[2] seem to be the reality of life in South Africa. Amnesty International reported in May 2010 on how corruption and nepotism impede access to housing and services in South Africa. It also mentioned "persistent poverty, rising levels of unemployment, and violent crime," and a "crisis in the public health sector."

Open Society's Criminal Justice Initiative has been running workshops on safety and security, youth at risk, drugs, dealing with the justice system, the effects of sentencing on the prison population, and preventing crime and violence, to mention just a few of its multitude of engagements. The human rights and governance program has been running workshops on HIV disclosure, education, access to information, and reducing electoral conflict. So far, these lofty aims have not been realized.

In 2010 Open Society South Africa launched the Open Society Monitoring Index to gauge "openness in society," since the desire for an "open society" is embedded in the South African constitution. It is interesting to note that, given the vicissitudes of life in crime-ridden South Africa, the Monitoring Index has attracted a large number of well-paid experts, round tables, and studies.

The Media Program has initiated several educational efforts for would-be journalists and broadcasters, as well as a baffling "Toolkit on Contemporary Issues in South Africa."

As Ivan Krastev observed, "Soros sees opportunities where others don't." In the case of South Africa, it is hard to see the opportunities. The country has not yet recovered from the atrocities of apartheid. Its Truth and Reconciliation Commission accepted that violence was inherent in the laws of the apartheid state and, crucially, it held individuals responsible only when their violent actions constituted crimes under apartheid laws.[3] By that logic, the judges at the Nuremberg Trials would not have been able to convict those who were "only following orders." As Martin Luther King said, "Violence begets violence."

IN 1997 OPEN SOCIETY established OSISA, a granting organization that works in ten countries in southern Africa: Angola, Botswana, Democratic Republic of the Congo, Lesotho, Malawi, Mozambique, Namibia, Swaziland, Zambia, and Zimbabwe. The foundations' expenditures in 2013 in this area were $32.6 million.

Another collection of countries lined up for Soros's assistance in eastern Africa, while Open Society's Initiative for West Africa included Senegal, Liberia, Sierra Leone, Ghana, Nigeria, Niger, Benin, and Côte d'Ivoire. The executive director of the West African Initiative is Abdul Tejan Cole, whom I had first met in Open Society's New York City offices. An attorney from Sierra Leone, he had been a member in the special court investigating crimes against humanity and a member of the anti-corruption commission.

Cole is an elegant, imposing figure, who fitted into New York's business world, although he struggled with a desire to go home to try to make a difference. This, despite his conviction that "progress and democracy are still out of reach" for West Africa. Too much blood has been shed.

Sierra Leone is one of the poorest countries in Africa, yet one of the richest in terms of natural resources. It has devastating poverty, but it also has famous diamond and gold mines and is a large producer of titanium and bauxite. Were it not for its collapsing governments[4] and the brutal ten-year war that killed thousands and displaced half the population, its citizens could be enjoying personal wealth. The ownership of natural resources and the fight for them often place populations at risk of violent conflict, autocratic governments, and corruption.

Aid was cut back long before the devastation, even from Canada, despite the direct connection between Nova Scotia's black population and Freetown, the ancestral home to many of the slaves who had escaped to Canada from the southern States. Civil war erupted in 1991 and lasted until 2002.

Two significant aspects of Sierra Leone's bloodletting have to be noted. All fighting groups systematically waged war on the civilian population, and they all engaged in the egregious abuse of children.[5] The use of child soldiers[6] was condemned by the United Nations, but the threats of trials for atrocities failed to discourage the warring sides. Entire villages were burned. Men's arms and legs were cut off. Women were routinely raped. Thousands were tortured, and authority figures were killed. Peace efforts failed as the Revolutionary United Front continued to attack towns even after its leader, Foday Sankoh, signed the peace agreements in 2000. The fighting destroyed all infrastructure, roads, schools, and civil society. Freetown was in ruins. The Revolutionary United Front gained support from Charles Taylor's National Patriotic Front in Liberia and used both Liberian and Burkinabe soldiers. The Special Court for Sierra Leone sentenced Charles Taylor to fifty years' incarceration for his role in the Sierra Leone civil war.

It was not until 2007 that Sierra Leone could finally conduct its first presidential and parliamentary elections.

Open Society supported the Truth and Reconciliation Commission to bring some sense of justice to those who had survived the conflict. Foday Sankoh, the leader of the ten-year terror campaign, died from a stroke while awaiting trial for his crimes. Several of his henchmen were indicted, but joined the fighting in Liberia instead, where most of them were killed. An astonishing $150 million was spent on the special courts, although ultimately they achieved little to assuage the wounds of Sierra Leoneans. What they did do, however, was to raise a number of interesting questions about criminal tribunals situated in the countries where the crimes had been committed. As in South Africa and Bosnia-Herzegovina, the victims and the perpetrators continue to live in the same country and are forced to see one another.

As Lansana Gberie, an academic and journalist who had worked in Liberia, wrote in his introduction to *Diamonds Without Maps*: "Diamonds have been at the centre of West Africa's nightmare … They helped to pay for former President Charles Taylor's rampage in Liberia and Côte d'Ivoire… Liberia became the major conduit for illicit diamonds from almost everywhere in Africa … billions of dollars' worth of stolen diamonds." Gberie did not think that the local truth commissions had done much to get people talking to each other again. What had, however, been accomplished was a successful campaign against "blood" or "conflict" diamonds. The hundreds of publications, the inquiries, and the dissertations had finally reached their goal with a worldwide ban on the use of illegally obtained diamonds. Gberie had worked for Partnership Africa Canada for four years, mainly on the diamond trade project.[7]

A large, round-faced man with a deceptively broad smile, Gberie was working at the United Nations when I last met him in 2012. He has a PhD from the University of Toronto, but rarely visits now. He is disappointed in Canada's declining international role. Some time ago, Canada was at the forefront of forcing change in West Africa. That is no longer the case.

Aryeh Neier talked of Sierra Leone and Liberia as two countries where much can be done with a little effort. They had both suffered in terrible civil wars — 250,000 people were killed in Liberia alone — but both are determined to change. Liberia has iron ore, diamonds, and gold.

Ellen Johnson Sirleaf, the current president of Liberia, is an old friend. He met her in 1985, the year that fourteen government leaders were lined up on the beach near Monrovia to be executed. "I got her out," Neier said, with uncharacteristic pride. Sirleaf became the first chairperson of the Open Society Initiative for West Africa. Now she is back home, he says, fighting corruption, nepotism, and the theft of the country's natural resources. She is the first woman head of state in Africa and the co-recipient of the 2011 Nobel Peace Prize for "the non-violent struggle for the safety of women and for women's rights to full participation in peace-building work."

In an interview in London, Sirleaf spoke about the need to return some land to the community. She has reduced Liberia's national debt, established the Truth and Reconciliation Commission, and allowed freedom of the press. She has focused on issues affecting women, started new healthcare programs, and brought funding to early childhood education. She has also clamped down on crime in the cities. In 2014 she was listed by *Forbes* as the seventieth most powerful woman in the world.

She insists that her cabinet show the same integrity that she herself has avowed, and Neier believes she is the one person who can force her colleagues to become accountable. Yet, as some of her former supporters say, members of her inner circle have already succumbed to the temptations offered by their positions and taken substantial bribes. At the end of her first term, even Sirleaf talked of the "mismanagement" of funds, of nepotism, and need to end corruption.

Sirleaf's sons hold high positions in the oil sector.

The rapid spread of the Ebola virus showed too many Liberians were still distrusted by their government. Even as Sirleaf appealed to all nations to help fight the epidemic, thousands of her own countrymen believed she was responsible for the devastation, that it was merely a ploy to exact more money from the international community.

IN AFRICA, the former colonial powers still flex their muscles in the countries they once occupied. There are 1.1 billion people living in African countries rich in resources. In most of those countries, the citizens live in penury while a tiny, well-connected elite reaps extraordinary benefits.

Equatorial Guinea has exported 400,000 barrels of oil a day since 1995. Its people live in abject poverty while the current ruler's son has built himself a mansion in Malibu and acquired a brace of speedboats, eight Ferraris, and a Maserati.[8]

Soros warned that "perhaps the greatest threat to freedom and democracy in the world today comes from the formation of unholy alliances between government and business." This danger is particularly visible in countries rich in natural resources.[9] Open Society established the West Africa Resource Watch Institute in Dakar, Senegal, where it trains advocates for accountability and transparency, including the Publish What You Pay campaigns that push companies to acknowledge what they pay for the natural resources that they extract. In 2002, Soros launched the Publish What You Pay coalition, a network of organizations with the same goals. In 2010 the value of minerals, oil, and gas from Africa was about $333 billion. The coalition has succeeded in convincing several companies to publish what they pay, giving civil society a chance to fight for the right to share in the revenues. Open Society has also supported Global Witness, an NGO that tries to persuade oil and mining companies to disclose all payments that they make to the governments where they operate.

Open Society is one of the funders of the Extractive Industries Transparency Initiative, and Anthony Richter from Open Society's New York office has served on its board. Since its founding in 2002, the British government, the World Bank, the IMF, and several other international bodies have come on board.

Africa has paid a high price for the world's energy consumption and its greed for diamonds and gold. Rivalries for riches cause conflicts that inflict even greater suffering on the poor. The extractive industries initiative was formed to try to get companies to disclose payments and to get governments, in turn, to disclose receipts.

In Ghana all contracts with foreign governments and corporations are now made public. Liberia, Niger, Nigeria, and Mozambique have all signed on, as have Norway, Mongolia, and Peru. In the Congo the war for possession of resources has been raging for decades. When lawyer George Washington Williams, the first black member of the Ohio state legislature, first spoke of "crimes against humanity" in 1890, he was referring to the atrocities committed by King Leopold's regime in what was then the Belgian Congo. In the nineteenth century, the human suffering arose out of a greed for resources, and little has changed since then. The Republic of Congo signed on to the Extractive Industries Transparency Initiative in February 2013, but some of the worst offenders have refused to join. In Zimbabwe President Robert Mugabe and his tight circle of supporters have been pillaging the country for decades. And while Nigeria has signed the agreement, it is an open secret that its vast oil wealth has failed to make its way down to its people. The Petroleum Industry Bill has been wending its way through the legislature with no end in sight. Corruption at every level is as great a problem now as it was before the transparency agreements.

Occasionally, the US government helps, as in the case of timber exports from Sierra Leone. "Eighteen members of the US Congress wrote to the State Department demanding it put pressure on the government of Sierra Leone," Tejan Cole told me.

As a Sierra Leonean, he is proud of the democratic elections, but he disagrees with the way some ministers were fired and others appeared out of nowhere. The new president, he thought, had already learned some bad habits from his predecessors

"The foundation pushes for peace and reconciliation. We try to end vicious cycles of an eye for an eye, before everyone ends up blind," he said. Both he and Tawanda Mutasah, Open Society's former director of transnational programs, spoke of the "big man" syndrome in Africa and how difficult it is to counter it. "Big men" set the rules and are impervious to laws. They are loved and admired by their followers. As an example, they both spoke of the problems in Kenya where two "big men," Uhuru Kenyatta and William Ruto, have vied in elections.

The International Criminal Court charged both men with inciting violence during the 2007 elections, though Ruto was appointed deputy president after Kenyatta won. They found it impossible to show up for their hearings while trying to keep the country calm after the terrorist attack on Nairobi. As the two former rivals faced trials at the International Criminal Court, they confirmed their alliance for the 2013 elections.

"We wanted six men to be charged in Kenya under international law, the rest to be tried at home," Tejan Cole said. "The convictions would signal the end of impunity. The fact that these 'big men' have had to present themselves at the International Criminal Court in The Hague is, already, a gain for justice."

Or is it? In reviewing the International Criminal Court's case files, it becomes obvious that a high proportion of those investigated and those already indicted — thirty indictments were outstanding as of the end of 2012 — were Africans. President Bashar al-Assad of Syria had not been indicted, as a result of Russian and Chinese opposition at the United Nations Security Council. None of the Security Council members — the United States, Russia, France, China, and the United Kingdom — is likely to agree to one of its nationals standing trial at the court, and while that situation persists, the court will always be viewed as biased.

The 2013 African Union summit protested that the International Criminal Court is disproportionately targeting Africans. The African Union's thirty-four members may yet withdraw from the Rome Statute, the agreement that established the International Criminal Court in 1998. Gberie, too, while he had no qualms about the specific people indicted, criticized the court for its focus on Africa. "It is not seen as just,"[10] he remarked, and that is a major failure.

Soros is one of the strongest supporters of the International Criminal Court.

SOROS WAS ALSO the most significant supporter of Jeffrey Sachs's "Millennium Villages" — an idea to solve the problem of poverty in

Africa. As special advisor to the secretary general of the United Nations, and the author of *The End of Poverty*, Sachs set himself the daunting task of eradicating poverty globally. After a five-year stint on Millennium Promises for the United Nations, he was able to convince Soros to come up with $120 million in seed money to launch his utopian Millennium Villages project — an experiment with African villagers in Kenya, Uganda, and Somalia.

Predictably, Sachs has failed to end poverty. Reading Nina Munk's book *The Idealist: Jeffrey Sachs and the Quest to End Poverty* reinforced my notion that Sachs's efforts — though often laudable in their aspirations and in their ability to extract significant sums in funding from others — have made the lives of those he touched worse, rather than better. With characteristic verve, he has denied that there is a reason for concern. He is sure that his "intellectual exercise" has succeeded because he has spread his theories about new methods of farming and distributed improved seeds, fertilizers, and millions of bed nets. In any event, he has been able to talk some nine or ten African countries into wanting his services.

As Istvan Rev, Soros's advisor and friend for about thirty years, told me, the Millennium Villages project has done nothing to change the world.

Corruption is still widespread in most of the African countries where Open Society funds have been spent, and the levels are not decreasing annually. The pillage of natural resources proceeds unabated as does the personal enrichment of those responsible and the misery of those who continue to have no protection. Open Society's James Stewart published a devastating report entitled *Corporate War Crimes* on the state of pillage in 2011.

In his op-ed piece in the *Financial Times* in March 2011, George Soros wrote that, "According to Nigeria's own corruption agency, up to $400 billion of oil money has been stolen or wasted over the past 50 years … The resource curse undermines the investment climate, raises costs for companies, threatens energy and mineral security, and consigns millions of citizens in resource-rich countries to poverty."

In its 2013 annual report, Global Witness, an environmental NGO, wrote that "over 70 percent of the world's biggest publicly listed extractive companies are now covered by transparency laws." The European Union signed on to the transparency rules and at the G8 summit in 2013, world leaders agreed to fast-track transparency laws in their own countries.

Joseph Bell, a director at International Senior Lawyers, told me that Soros was personally involved in Liberia, Sierra Leone, and Guinea. He has backed both economic development and the push for the rule of law in Africa. "His ideas and ideals are often underappreciated. He is an intellectual who wants to make an impact," Bell said. "If you scratch under any serious cause in Washington," he added, "you are likely to find Soros's hand."

Open Society's expenditures in Africa in 2013 were $82 million.

THIRTEEN

Myanmar: Another Test for Democracy

Burma, renamed Myanmar by the army after a military coup in 1962, has witnessed such a profound sea change since 2011, the year the dictatorship ended, that visiting tourists can hardly believe it ever existed. Visitors have been flooding to the country since then, and Lonely Planet lists Myanmar among its top ten tourist destinations.

While some residents are still living in fear, suspicious that the generals are waiting for their chance to arrest everyone and return to the past, others are noisily celebrating their freedom. For many years, human rights organizations were barred from entering Myanmar, demonstrations were brutally put down, and prisoners were beaten and often killed in custody. Nationwide protests in 1988 and 2007 were followed by vicious crackdowns.

Perhaps the most visible difference in recent years has been the reappearance of Nobel Peace Prize laureate Aung San Suu Kyi, who spent most of the past two decades under house arrest. She is the daughter of Aung San, one of Burma's best remembered national heroes and the man who led the country to independence from British rule. He died mere months before it was finally achieved.

Whereas being caught with a photograph of Suu Kyi in early 2011 would have guaranteed a long jail sentence, today there are posters of her all over Rangoon. Whereas mentioning her very existence used to be tempting fate, now she has won a seat in parliament. The generals were even willing to accept the results of the March 2012 election that put forty new members from The National League for Democracy into the military-dominated parliament.

Suu Kyi spoke to her supporters about the triumph of the people and the beginning of a new era. She travelled to Thailand and Europe, where she was welcomed as a survivor of a peaceful struggle against military rule, and to the United States in September 2012, where she was presented with Congress's highest award, the Congressional Gold Medal. Meanwhile, Myanmar announced a new round of prisoner releases. By September almost all political prisoners had been set free. The government lifted media restrictions, and NGOs were allowed back into the country.

When I first met him, Neier talked of Suu Kyi with great warmth. She had won the national elections in 1990, but had been prevented from taking office. Open Society had supported the entire family and set up its Burma Project in 1993. Neier had personally known Suu Kyi since 1996 when his daughter studied Tibetan history under her husband, Michael Aris, who was a Tibetan scholar. In 1999 Suu Kyi could not travel abroad to be with her dying husband during his final days because the regime would have prevented her from returning. Neier visited her in Rangoon in 1996 and again in 2002, two of the few times when she was allowed visitors. She had, he told me, become a personal friend.

Human Rights Watch accused security forces in Myanmar of fomenting ethnic violence. Open Society has condemned the continued use of forced labour and asked questions about the fate of the "disappeared." In the past, the military had spread land mines throughout the areas adjacent to Thailand, which belong to the Karen people, an ethnic minority, but it was not until 2012 that the president admitted the country needed help clearing them. Until then, they could not be discussed, even when people lost limbs in explosions.

Neier had predicted the 2011 loosening of the military's hold in Myanmar as a perfect opportunity for Open Society to support local NGOs. It was the kind of well-timed entry that OS has favoured throughout the years: the ability to mobilize funds quickly when an opportunity presents itself.

In 2011 Open Society spent more than $10 million on its Burma Project/Indonesia/Southeast Asia Initiative to document human rights abuses. In *The Philanthropy of George Soros,* Chuck Sudetic devotes an entire chapter to Burma, which he describes as "one of the richest countries" in Southeast Asia.

The Central Bank is now independent and rushing reforms to welcome foreign investment. Both the International Monetary Fund and the World Bank are in Myanmar with an aid package of US$245 million, according to the journal *Foreign Affairs.* Foreign leaders, including Tony Blair and Barack Obama, have visited U Thein Sein, the president who was hand-picked by his fellow generals in 2010. *Business Monitor* has published a special report examining Myanmar's "emerging investment story" while the Institute for Human Rights and Business announced a new multiyear project to ensure that new investments are "consistent with international human rights standards."

In January 2013, Soros met with the leaders of the 88 Generation Students, many of whom had been imprisoned by the previous regime. The group named itself after the 1988 uprising against military rule. Soros asked how the transition to a democratic system could be speeded up and offered to bring experts in to teach transparency and accountability to provide a better business climate for foreign investors.

"I told him that without peace, this country cannot have democracy," said Khun Htun Oo, a Shan, who met with Soros at a round table with ethnic minority leaders in Rangoon. While the new government has engineered peace with some of the minorities, it has not yet negotiated with all of them. Worse, Suu Kyi has refrained from speaking about the plight of the Karen, Shan, Kachin, Rohingya, and other minorities who are still subject to random arrests and casual harassment by the military and feel a justified sense of powerlessness. In 2012 armed Rakhine Buddhists attacked Rohingya homes, killing hundreds of people. Entire villages were razed.

In May 2013 Suu Kyi first met with leaders of the United Nationalities Alliance, the group representing all minorities in Myanmar. She discussed the possibility — although not the probability — of constitutional amendments that would give the minorities more say in parliament. That, for now, is highly unlikely. After all, this is the same constitution, cobbled together by the military, that bars Suu Kyi from ever assuming the presidency.

The military, long beneficiaries of the trade in rubies, which are found mostly in areas settled by minorities, are unlikely to abide by changes that could threaten their own entitlements.

Open Society's Burma Project/Indonesia/Southeast Asia Initiative's website declares support for "marginalized groups." Its "featured work" includes a photograph of exiled Rohingya and a story on a "blood rubies" exhibition, "as a way of telling the story of human rights abuses in Burma." So far, there are no signs that Myanmar will support transparency in resource extraction or distributing a fair share of the wealth to its population.

Opposition leader Suu Kyi, while decrying the violence, seems to have decided that maintaining her deal with the military is the only hope she has of getting to the president's office. She has followed a route of assigning blame equally to Buddhists and Muslims and talking about "the rule of law," rather than pointing a finger at the obvious aggressors. On Armed Forces Day she sat in the front row for the march past, right next to the high ranks.[1]

Human Rights Watch has criticized her speeches and *The New York Times* has remarked that she has been "tragically silent" on the persecution of Rakhine Muslims. In 2013 Human Rights Watch published its 153-page report on the ethnic cleansing of Rohingya Muslims in Burma's Arakan state. On January 13, 2014, more than forty men, women, and children were massacred in in the Rohingya Muslim area of Myanmar. As the violence escalated there has been a sharp increase of refugees in neighbouring states.

The New York Times reported that "Suu Kyi has defended her lack of action to the foreign news media, saying that taking sides could further exacerbate tensions, an explanation that even her Western supporters believe is calculated to avoid offending voters ahead of elections next year."[2]

The National League for Democracy, the party Suu Kyi helped found, held its first national congress in March 2013. It has won overwhelming victories in forty by-elections and is set to gain power in the next election. There were few new faces at the congress, despite Suu Kyi's announcement that the party needed new blood. Most of those in attendance had served long prison terms for belonging to the same party whose existence they were now celebrating without military intervention.

The Twenty-Second World Economic Forum on East Asia was hosted in Myanmar in June 2013, and the Association of Southeast Asian Nations Summit followed in May 2014. But even Open Society agrees that the country still has a long way to go in reforming its judiciary, building infrastructure, and making sure that its resources do not become a "curse." Most of Myanmar's natural resources are still untapped. There are not only rubies, jade, and sapphires, but also nickel, chromium, silver, and zinc. The sales from Myanmar's Gems Emporium in one month of 2013 amounted to $702 billion.

During a 2013 Italian interview, Soros mentioned that the environment is now a subject very close to his heart and the rush to riches could endanger more of Myanmar's fragile forests and water: "I think considerable progress is being made in dealing with the management of natural resources. I am particularly involved in Myanmar, where land-grabbing is a big problem." He added that the government was responding to the need for reforms.

Meanwhile, a group led by Soros bid for the Myanmar mobile network licence in May 2013 and lost.

In late 2014 Soros supported the Myanmar government's push for more foreign investment. He had already personally invested several million dollars through the SPA Group of companies. "We would be eager to do it [invest] in the areas of banking, finance, and agriculture. This is where we feel the country, the people, need this investment most," Soros said.[3]

The next few years will determine whether Myanmar is heading in the right direction, but today the country is still very far from the kind of open society Soros has spent his millions to promote. Suu Kyi's National League for Democracy Party will participate in the process, but she is still barred from running for office.

FOURTEEN

Tackling America

I n *The Age of Fallibility*, Soros identified one of the shortcomings of American society as "an excessive admiration for success — measured in monetary terms — to the detriment of more intrinsic values." When his Open Society Foundations first became active in the United States in the early nineties, he decided that they would focus their attention on "intrinsic values" by concentrating on ethical issues that involved medicine and the law.

Soros's first initiative was the Project on Death in America, which promoted better palliative and end-of-life care services. His second initiative focused on drug addiction, in the context of "harm reduction." In his definition, "harm" included both the harm caused by illegal drugs and the harm caused by America's war on drugs. "I found myself enmeshed in a problem area in which prejudice and intolerance are at the worst," he wrote in *The Age of Fallibility*.

In 1996 Aryeh Neier hired Gara LaMarche to devise a way that Open Society could lessen inequality in the United States. Neier's interest was in ensuring access to equal justice for all Americans. LaMarche was the ideal person to promote these ideas on behalf of Open Society because he had experience both in public health and, as executive director of the

Texas Civil Liberties Union, in crime and punishment. When he arrived in Texas in 1984, the state proudly maintained its traditions of the harshest sentences and the largest per capita prison population in the United States. His approach to changing the system was simple. He set out to persuade the government that the high rate of incarceration made no fiscal sense. He presented himself as a fellow conservative, but even in the tough economic times of the eighties, he was unable to convince the insiders that his proposals made sense. What he was able to do was to take his ideas to New York.

President Clinton's 1996 decision to end benefits for legal immigrants stirred Soros to take a hard look at the plight of new arrivals in America. Perhaps it was Soros's own immigrant story that drew him to oppose this new legislation. "I got $50 million [from Soros] to create a program fast," LaMarche said. "In three weeks, we announced the 'Emma Lazarus Fund,' named after nineteenth-century poet Emma Lazarus whose poem, 'The New Colossus,' is inscribed on a plaque on the Statue of Liberty where it welcomes immigrants."[1] Her words are quoted by American schoolchildren: "Give me your tired, your poor … " The fund would pay the costs of citizenship applications, help provide English-language instruction, and assist in efforts, both in the courts and through public education, to gain naturalization. The issue, as Soros explained, was one of justice or equal treatment for all, regardless of immigration status.

Meanwhile, the foundation's attention shifted to pretrial incarceration in the United States, the inequality of the bail system, the long sentences for victimless crimes, and the dominant presence of the poor in US jails. It was predictable that LaMarche and Herb Sturz, the genius at Open Society who has helped so many underdogs, would become friends and allies with common interests. And unlike many of the foundation's programs, this one is still an ongoing effort.[2]

LaMarche left behind several projects that had not yet run their course when he left the foundation. "George," LaMarche said, "likes to end things. He prefers to fund something that is expected to end within a reasonable length of time. Soros's own dynamics are restlessness, the exact opposite of how other foundations work." It's a way of thinking that has served Soros well in the financial world: Get in, get out, and never overstay. Matthew Bishop and Michael Green have called the business-style approach to philanthropy "philanthrocapitalism."[3] Soros, like other philanthrocapitalists, has tended to focus on results: "The impact that giving has."

When I last saw LaMarche, he occupied a small office at New York University's Wagner School of Public Service. Since then, he has joined the Democracy Alliance as its president. The American right steadfastly refers to the Democracy Alliance as a "shadowy, left-wing organization," because Soros has been one of its donors since the alliance's beginnings in 2005. It defines itself as "a partnership of changemakers who are committed to a stronger democracy and a more progressive America."

Open Society Institute Baltimore was launched in 1998 as a five-year program, but it has been repeatedly extended, as its impact became obvious. It was to be a kind of field office for testing ideas and strategies to deal with the oppressive problems of poverty and the lack of civic engagement. More than $50 million was spent on projects to boost reading and math scores in public schools and on after-school programs. Open Society Baltimore's website declares that the root causes of the city's problems are drug addiction, the overuse of incarceration, and obstacles that stand in the way of youth succeeding both in and out of school. The question of how the Baltimore office set about solving these problems led me to Diana Morris.

When we met in 2012, Morris was acting director of all US Programs, a temporary assignment that she was keen to complete so she could stop the weekly commute from Baltimore. There was a large photograph of her young daughter on her formal, well-organized desk. A friendly person with a compact build, she was elegantly dressed for a day in the office. She had an open smile, but like many of Open Society's staff, she remained guarded during our conversation.

She told me that the board expected more of the American programs, and Soros himself wanted to see additional campaigns that would draw attention to individual social issues. He likes campaigns because they have a specific aim and trajectory. Irrespective of the amounts he is willing to give, or how fine and beneficial the cause, Soros "dislikes open-ended programs," she said, reiterating LaMarche's point.

When she described this aspect of Soros's charitable activities, I had the distinct impression that Morris didn't believe that the nature of her own commitments allowed for such a closed or fixed approach. The idea that incarceration rates would drop by 50 percent as a result of Open Society's Justice Initiative seems like a long-term dream rather than a target for a ten-year plan.

Nor is it likely that equality of opportunity — one of the buzz phrases in this Open Society office — can be achieved in our lifetimes, let alone in a predictable time frame. In the United States there are approximately 2.3 million inmates in jails. In addition, there are almost 1 million youths in juvenile detention. A very large percentage of them are black, Hispanic, and Native American. The injustice of this is one of the reasons why the Open Society Foundation launched its initiative to change US drug laws.

While the Campaign for Black Male Achievement, begun in 2008, will undoubtedly have its heroes and small gains in places like Milwaukee and Baltimore, measuring its impact will likely remain as elusive as its mottos of "ensuring that black boys have the opportunity to excel academically" or "strengthening low income families through responsible fatherhood initiatives." What may be accomplished within the time frame is to locate some willing partners who will stay the course, after Open Society has moved on to another campaign.

In 2011 the Open Society Campaign for Black Male Achievement partnered with Root Cause to launch a leadership and sustainability institute. It joined fifty-one other programs in support of black males in the United States. The majority of black men in that country still fail in the educational system and almost 30 percent of them still serve time in US jails. It is too soon to know whether the different approach taken by the campaign will be effective. I assume it will align with the foundations' other programs of educating elites who can serve as role models.

In Baltimore the challenges continue: reducing incarceration times for drug abusers, reforming operations at the city's drug-treatment centres, and finding ways to help inner city kids discover options not rooted in hopelessness and petty crime. Crime rates in Baltimore, where the vast majority of prisoners are black men charged with drug possession, have not declined significantly since the foundation has been operating there.

"We try to do systemic change," Morris said, echoing other Open Society executives. "We work with public agencies and we do not need to take credit for what we do. This approach, I have found, adds another incentive for others to work with us."

In 2010 Soros decided the Baltimore office should fundraise as a "validation of its work." It was tough to explain to others that a billionaire needed additional cash, but the benefit of being surrounded by people who believe in the lasting value of their work is that they set about fundraising. The aim was $20 million, and "we raised $15 million in the first year," Morris said with some justified pride, "from corporations but also from individuals." In some ways, it has been a measure of success or at least a measure of appreciation. Morris's work, painstakingly long hours, and small, incremental gains do not lend themselves to easy closure.

Nor do Herb Sturz's myriad projects, although in his case it barely matters because he usually seems able find someone to carry on the work after the initial funding has run dry. He created the After-School Corporation in 1998, in response to Soros's desire to "do something for New York City."[4] It was hardly a new idea for Sturz, but it was new to Soros. The idea was to found a program to keep kids occupied and fed after school, whether their parents were working or chronically out of work and out of luck. The program would be run in partnership with small-scale community organizations and, ultimately, by the Board of Education and the city itself. Soros helped kick-start the program with $125 million. Funding is now close to triple that figure, and it serves more than 40,000 children, providing reasonable snacks, cutting street crime, and giving working parents some time off from caring for their kids. As Sturz, ever the optimist, expected, others — both private and public — kicked in to help grow the programs. Even the Ford Foundation is now engaged. Sturz's goal is to make after-school programs universally available in the United States.

Recently, Sturz has succeeded in connecting this program with his ReServe project, which places skilled retirees in part-time positions with social service or government organizations that can't afford to hire regular staff. The program pays a nominal ten dollars an hour because,

Sturz says, being paid gives people a sense of pride in their work and in some cases the extra money helps. ReServe may take years to establish itself. Innovative social programs rarely take root in the way that Soros prefers — with a set time limit. Nor is it easy to find other funders when Soros is already involved.

In 2013 Open Society spent more than $200 million of its approximately $1 billion in the United States. That does not include Soros's personal contributions to political campaigns. During the past thirty years, Open Society has spent $1.2 billion to promote reform in the United States on issues such as criminal justice, drug-related sentencing, immigration, and democratic governance.

HAD SOROS CONTINUED to spread his billions from Russia to Azerbaijan, Poland to Sierra Leone, and Myanmar to Bosnia, he would likely have stayed out of the spotlight for American conservatives. His foundations would certainly have failed to attract the attentions of Fox News, Bill O'Reilly, and Rush Limbaugh. While he might still have been one of the most hated men in central Europe — where he has done a great deal to improve people's lives — he would not have become a pariah in Republican circles.

But of course, given Soros's predilection for ignoring his critics and choosing his own enemies, it was inevitable that he would take an interest in the United States' belligerent foreign policies after 9/11. He denounced President Bush's War on Terror and the "pursuit of American supremacy," a pursuit that he believed had led to an erosion of American power and influence. It is, maintains Soros, as impossible to wage a war on terror as it is to wage war on fear, but words can, and often do, persuade people that an idea, no matter how impossible, is reality.

With a few of his fellow billionaires,[5] he set up a fund to defeat George W. Bush's 2004 run for a second term in the White House. Soros's contribution to the America Coming Together fund was about to $27 million.[6] At the time, Soros described this effort in *Commentary* as "the central project of my life" and "a matter of life and death."

He argued that the United States could sacrifice its principles of democracy and the rule of law if pushed by clever operatives, such as Vice

President Dick Cheney and Secretary of Defense Donald Rumsfeld. It was a game in which George W. Bush may have been "an unwitting tool."

Contemplating the aftermath of 9/11, Soros realized that there was a fundamental error in Karl Popper's theory that critical thinking would lead to a clearer understanding of reality. In a democracy, where all political claims can receive a hearing, it was relatively easy to manipulate public opinion. "Techniques of deception" developed in advertising and marketing were equally useful when selling a president. The amount of money spent in advertising — mainly television — could appeal to Americans' emotions in a way that a reasoned, logical argument would not. Thus, he argued, the radical right had captured the Republican Party and "using 9/11 as a pretext, took over the levers of power." The fear and insecurity Americans felt after 9/11 had, Soros said, been exploited by Bush's circle, "led to the invasion of Iraq on false pretenses, and violated established standards of human rights in pursuing terrorists." Labelling all opposition as unpatriotic, the Bush administration was able to dupe Americans into an unnecessary war.

In his book *The Bubble of American Supremacy*, Soros wrote that no one knows yet the real motives behind the Iraqi invasion, but the truth about private interests and public gullibility was beginning to emerge, although only on the graves of the thousands of dead Americans and the uncounted Iraqis who have perished in an inexplicable conflict. In *The Age of Fallibility,* he went further, writing, "The main obstacle to a stable and just world order is the United States." He saw the Bush agenda as highly nationalistic, emphasizing the use of force, rather than international cooperation. He identified three destructive forces in George W. Bush's America: "market fundamentalism, religious fundamentalism, and the neoconservative advocacy of American supremacy." The three schools of thought coalesced only in their desire for power.

"A more profound rethinking of America's role in the world is needed," he wrote.[7] Such fighting words were bound to attract a vengeful response then, and they have continued to do so ever since.

"For traditional-minded Americans, George Soros is public enemy number one," proclaimed Bill O'Reilly, Fox News Channel's political commentator, in his bestselling book *Culture Warrior*. In 2006, David

Horowitz, founder of the conservative journal *FrontPage Mag,* and Richard Poe published *The Shadow Party: How George Soros, Hillary Clinton, and Sixties Radicals Seized Control of the Democratic Party.* The book claimed that "radical infiltrators have been quietly transforming America's societal, cultural, and political institutions … From their perches in the Democratic hierarchy, they seek to undermine the war on terror, destabilize the nation, and effect radical 'regime change' in America."

Both Poe and Horowitz were already *New York Times* bestselling authors with some credibility, and their claims were not entirely without foundation. Soros had called the United States a destabilizing force and claimed that "the main enemy of open society is no longer the communist but the capitalist threat." Those were fighting words, and they brought the battle to Soros's doorstep. But portraying George Soros as the "Lenin" behind the "Shadow Party," a man whose ideas are as dangerous to America as those of the 9/11 perpetrators, was sheer overstatement. *Boston Globe* columnist Alex Beam's cheerful declaration that Soros is "a greater threat to democracy" than Rupert Murdoch was in the same category. Scott Shore of *Intellectual Conservative* called Soros a "soft-money Marxist," whatever that means. He is *FrontPage Mag's* "radical, anti-American billionaire." An antagonistic daily online newsfeed records his latest moves. Republican media darling Ann Coulter rarely misses an opportunity to attack him, and *Human Events* readers have voted him the "single most destructive leftist demagogue in the country."

But, as Leon Botstein said, Soros is fearless. He can't be intimidated.

AS THE CATASTROPHIC consequences of the crash of 2008 continued, Soros was quick to blame the United States for the worldwide recession. In his 2008 book, *The New Paradigm for Financial Market: The Credit Crisis of 2008 and What It Means,* he returned to his theories of reflexivity as it related to the financial markets. With the evidence of the brutal bust following the unrealistic super boom, the bankruptcy of Lehman Brothers, the AIG bailout, and the merger of Merrill Lynch and the Bank of America, it was time to take another hard look at Soros's ideas.

Unlike previous crashes, this one spread far and wide. Today's capital markets didn't recognize borders and were governed entirely by greed. "The worldwide financial system was unstable because it was built on the false premise that financial markets can be left to their own devices." Those who were wedded to that concept believed that markets would always find their own equilibrium. That theory, Soros said, was false.

Soros criticized the Federal Reserve's unsuccessful attempts to pour salve onto the gaping wounds left by the crash. His new paradigm states that relying on the markets to correct themselves does not work. He condemned complex financial instruments, such as collateralized debt obligations, and declared that these new financial toys demand complex controls. He said that those who make decisions for the economy in the United States must realize that the market is neither efficient nor predictable. If we ignore that, we are facing a "self-reinforcing decline."

New thinking was needed. It included his theory on what causes "bubbles" and how to predict them, something the economists and financial analysts failed to do in the years preceding the crash. He argued that both the "rational expectations" theory and the "efficient markets hypothesis" crumbled with the events of 2008. He accused "market fundamentalists" of wilful blindness and a lack of moral backbone. Chicago economist Milton Friedman's "intellectual underpinning for two decades of financial deregulation"[8] had wrought havoc with people's savings and almost destroyed the financial system.

"The bankruptcy of Lehman [Brothers] was also the bankruptcy of prevailing economic theory," Soros told an audience in Hainan, China, in April 2013. He then went on to tout his much-repeated theory of reflexivity, before returning to the subject at hand. People's biases and actions when they participate in the market will affect the market's reality. Far from supply and demand neatly balancing each other, the perceptions of individuals and groups can change the reality they experience. It was clear that Soros believed his theory of reflexivity had finally caught up with the realities of the financial markets.

Rather than hide from the campaign of vilification, Soros and his foundations kept up their criticism of the US government, even under Barack Obama's presidency. The unbridled greed that affected American society had existed long before Obama came to the White House, and Obama had inherited rather than created the crash. But the new president had no quick fixes for the economy.

During the 2012 Republican race, Newt Gingrich used Soros's name to demean Mitt Romney, then the front runner: "I think for most Republican voters, the idea of trying to nominate a Soros-approved candidate is not a very appealing idea."

Needless to say, Soros had never "approved" Romney, but the allegation itself may have been enough to drive a few conservative votes away from him. The attacks were, as Gara LaMarche noted, "characterized by innuendo, guilt-by-association, and questioning of our patriotism — all classic McCarthy techniques."

"He breeds resentment," according to Soros's longest-serving director, Istvan Rev.

It is interesting to compare the vilification of Soros to the milder resentment that the Republican Koch brothers inspire. *The Economist* calculated the annual turnover of Koch Industries at around $115 billion. The brothers' estimated wealth as of 2014 is calculated to be $40.6 billion, and they are sixth on *Forbes'* billionaires list while George Soros is merely twenty-fourth.

They have also taken an active role in US elections. They announced publicly that they would spend whatever it took to rid America of the socialist menace represented by President Obama and his leftish supporters. They are libertarians; they object to government oversight of private enterprise; and they are true believers in markets finding their own equilibrium.

The Kochs spent about $400 million through a range of foundations, such as Freedom Partners, to defeat Obama in 2012. They failed, but they are unlikely to accept another Democrat in the White House without a fight.[9]

Meanwhile, in 2012 George Soros donated $1 million to the Super PAC[10] that helped fund Obama's rise to the top. "If anyone can lead the country in the right direction, it is Obama," Soros said. He had great hopes for this presidency, although he doubted that anyone could fulfill all the promises that Obama carried with him to the White House. As it turned out, Obama disappointed both the American public and Soros personally.

There was little cause for celebration in liberal circles when it became obvious that Obama's government preferred targeted killings as a way of dealing with America's enemies rather than the more difficult and legally fraught methods of the previous administrations: extradition, imprisonment, Guantánamo, and torture. By the end of October 2013, the US military had killed more than 3,000 foreign nationals, most in Pakistan, Yemen, and Somalia. The use of drones had rendered the killing both distant and seemingly bloodless.

Obama's election promises about closing Guantánamo remained only that. Promises. As Human Rights Watch's Kenneth Roth argued in *The New York Times Book Review*, not much has changed since the second Bush term as far as the "war on terror" goes. Only the words have changed. The administration doesn't use those words anymore. Americans do not necessarily feel safer, and it is difficult to claim that civilian populations are friendlier to the United States in countries where drones have been used. Jihad against the West has neither diminished, nor been much weakened as a result of the CIA's activities, and it is hard to imagine that it will end in some sort of international peace agreement. Osama Bin Laden may be dead, but his followers are very much alive and wreaking havoc in ever broader spheres. The Islamic State became a greater threat to peace in the Middle East than Al Qaeda.

In 2013 Soros joined the Super PAC advocating Hillary Clinton as the next president of the United States, although she has not yet agreed to run for office. Soros has assumed the role of co-chair of the Super PAC's national finance committee.

In its March 2014 report, the New York Public Interest Group revealed that Soros and his wife had given $1 million to the New York State Democratic Committee. Soros was, by far, the biggest donor.

As he wrote in *The Age of Fallibility*, "changing the attitude and policies of the United States remains my top priority."

FIFTEEN

And Justice for All

In 2013 Open Society spent $248 million on rights and justice and $285 million on governance and accountability, by far the two biggest single items on its list of expenditures.

James Goldston is the executive director of Open Society's Justice Initiative. He is a Columbia and Harvard Law School graduate who has litigated several groundbreaking cases before the European Court of Human Rights. From 2007 to 2008, he served as Coordinator of Prosecutions and Senior Trial Attorney in the Office of the Prosecutor at the International Criminal Court. Prior to joining Open Society, he had been legal director at the European Roma Rights Centre, the director general for the European Union's Mission to Bosnia-Herzegovina, and had worked in the office of the US Attorney for the southern district of New York, where he specialized in the prosecution of organized crime.

Goldston is in his forties, slim, fit, dark haired, with a firm handshake and an attitude of confident preoccupation with whatever pieces of his daily puzzle have been abandoned to make time for my interruptions. I first met him in November 2011 and then again in 2012. The first time he had just flown in from Sierra Leone and Nigeria and was on his way to Paris and The Hague. "We brought a case against Nigeria for giving

Taylor asylum and the Nigerian government had to let him go,"[1] he said with obvious delight.

The murderous career of Charles Taylor, president of Liberia from 1997 to 2003, has been well documented. By the time he was forced out of office, he had devastated the country and left millions of dysfunctional citizens behind him. He was born in 1948 into a family of freed slaves, the group who founded Liberia in the nineteenth century. After studying in the United States, he returned to Liberia to work for Samuel Doe's corrupt regime, then fell out with Doe and launched a rebellion against the government.

A born showman, Taylor was flamboyant and overconfident, an imaginative dresser who strutted the world stage wearing military uniforms or quasi-African traditional costumes with equal flair. He was also one of the most brutal warlords in Africa. His Revolutionary United Front used child soldiers, committed mass atrocities, and raped and murdered villagers in Sierra Leone and Liberia. The obvious reason for Taylor's war was to secure sole access to the world's single largest deposit of diamonds.

Goldston had brought the case against him before the UN-backed Special Court for Sierra Leone, held at the International Criminal Court. The trial started on January 6, 2008.

"The accused has been found responsible for aiding and abetting some of the most heinous crimes in human history," Judge Richard Lussick said at the end of the trial in April 2012. Taylor was sentenced to fifty years in prison, the first conviction in a court known for its foot-dragging prosecutions.

It was the first time since the post–Second World War Nuremberg Trials that a head of state had been found guilty by an international court. The judgement sends a clear message "that powerful leaders who perpetrate atrocities to gain or retain power can one day be held responsible." This is good news for those who are engaged in human rights work, but not necessarily good news for countries that value their own judiciary above that of any other.

The International Criminal Court, defined as "the first permanent, treaty-based, international criminal court to help end impunity for the perpetrators of the most serious crimes ..." was established by the United

Nations' Rome Statutes of 1998 and ratified over the next several years. Its objectives, as laid out by its founding statutes, were to prosecute "genocide, crimes against humanity and war crimes." It was an ambitious goal that has so far remained mostly elusive. As of December 2012, 121 countries have signed the "Statute of the Court," meaning they recognize its authority. If a country has not signed, its citizens cannot be tried at the court. Unsurprisingly, many of the countries most infamous for human rights violations have stayed away. Each member of the UN Security Council can veto an attempt by the court to bring someone to trial, and governments in power can simply refuse to give up their nationals under indictment.

The United States has not signed the Rome Statutes. It is not about to surrender its right to try its own citizens or the citizens of any other country who have committed crimes against the United States or its citizens. While the United States has pushed for international jurisdiction in atrocities, it has opposed all attempts to have the law apply to itself and has sought guarantees that no American soldier would ever be indicted by an international court.[2] As Courtney Griffiths, Taylor's defence lawyer argued, convictions in the International Criminal Court set a dangerous precedent: British prime ministers and American presidents could be charged for their involvement in places such as Afghanistan and Iraq.

Canadian author and journalist George Jonas goes even further than that: "The court derives its power from no source of discernible legitimacy. It is designed to be a law unto itself. The judges and prosecutors are unelected officials arrogating jurisdiction to themselves across all lines of national sovereignty."[3] In Jonas's view, special interest groups have taken control of the court as a way of meting out justice against those of whom they disapprove.

For the first ten years of its existence, only ten cases were brought to trial and only one person was convicted. Among those tried was Congolese warlord Thomas Lubanga who had recruited child soldiers to fight in his Union of Congolese Patriots militia. The children were taken from schools, beaten, and drugged until they were deemed fit for battle. One hundred and twenty-nine child victims participated in his trial. Lubanga was sentenced to fourteen years. Goldston considers the case vital to show that there is no impunity. Sadly, the International Criminal Court lacks the capacity to try more than a few perpetrators at any one time. While Thomas Lubanga's conviction shows that the court has some teeth, Lubanga's fellow murderers and rapists are still at large. Local courts seem to lack the fortitude to try cases. Thus perpetrators can be reasonably sure of reaching a comfortable old age before justice catches up with them.

The International Criminal Court has been unable to bring Omar Hassan Al-Bashir, the genocidal ruler of Sudan, anywhere near a court of justice, although it has indicted Al-Bashir on a range of charges, most of them perpetrated in the Darfur region. Al-Bashir's intent to commit genocide became clear with his well-coordinated attacks on the 2,450,000 civilians who found a haven in the refugee camps. "Al-Bashir organized the destitution, insecurity, and harassment of the survivors. He did not need bullets. He used other weapons: rape, hunger, and fear. As efficient, but silent," said the prosecutor. Yet Al-Bashir is welcomed by other African rulers, who are successfully thumbing their noses at the court.

Goldston, like Soros, does not think that the International Criminal Court has fulfilled in its mandate, but he is pleased with its general direction. It may not have achieved much in terms of convictions, but it encourages countries with local courts to carry on with local trials.

Open Society Justice has supported the establishment of mobile courts in eastern Congo, which is the site of mass sexual violence carried out with utter impunity by the army, rebels, militias, and others. The courts have the discretion to hear other cases, but the majority of appeals to the system have come from victims of rape.

In 2013 the court's new set of judges and its new Gambian chief prosecutor, Fatou Bensouda, faced the challenges of catching up with the complex issues of existing cases. Meanwhile Goldston remained determined to continue pushing them to do their job more effectively.

Perhaps the most newsworthy case before the court recently was that of Kenyan President Uhuru Kenyatta and Deputy President William Ruto. Both were charged with inciting the violence that almost ended in civil war near the time of the 2007 elections. More than one thousand people were killed and many more were wounded in what was seen as tribal violence, incited by the leaders of each faction. Since the charges were laid, however, Kenyatta has been doing a good job as president, travelling abroad to foster relations with the United Kingdom and the World Bank. The local economy is recovering, and the Nairobi papers have been attacking the International Criminal Court for proceeding with its prosecutions. In September 2013 the two former adversaries came together for a common response to the Islamist attack on the Westgate shopping mall in Nairobi. Though a signatory to the Rome Statutes, Kenya has repeatedly attacked the court and its mandate since the case against its two leaders began. The tactics have exposed the court's weakness: it cannot compel member states to fulfill their obligations.

The Justice Initiative's lofty aims include forcing accountability for international crimes, countering corruption, carrying out justice reform, putting in place legal remedies for bribery, and spreading the need for freedom of expression and information: "Using law to protect and empower people ... through litigation, advocacy, research, technical assistance."

In some countries, Goldston explained, pretrial detention can take longer than whatever sentence the court may eventually award for the crime itself. Open Society has recently published a global survey entitled *Presumed Guilty: The Global Overuse of Pretrial Detention.*

There are thousands of cases where people have awaited trials for more than a dozen years, and in some countries intimidation and torture are routine police procedures. Unable to pay bribes, make bail, or hire lawyers, millions languish in jails with no clean water, no medical staff, and no medications. Outbreaks of infectious diseases in overcrowded holding cells have killed off more prisoners than old-fashioned executions. The average length of pretrial detention in the European Union is five and a half months. In Nigeria, it is four years. Goldston has done fieldwork in law reform in more than thirty countries, in Africa, Asia, and Europe.

To speed up the process, Goldston has suggested that Open Society would fund paralegals. In Sierra Leone, where there are only 100 lawyers for three million people, paralegals can help resolve civil disputes and hold government officials accountable for abusing prisoners. In societies where the average person has scant knowledge of his or her rights, paralegals can inform the most vulnerable.

Among the issues that Goldston has aggressively pursued is Roma integration in Czech schools. As a result, the 2007 European Court judgement ordered the Czech Republic to eliminate the segregation of Roma children into separate classes. Unfortunately, the Czechs have ignored the court. Given the way the French have been dealing with Roma refugees, the court hardly seems to have a basis for charging the Czechs alone. Yet Goldston is optimistic: "The level of subjugation the Roma have experienced cannot be eliminated in twenty years. Attitudes run too deep, [they're] too ingrained, but there has been some slow progress. The courts have affirmed that Roma are entitled to human rights."[4]

In response to the 2010 World Cup bombing in Kampala, Uganda, governments in the region have cracked down on opposition parties, human rights NGOs, and lawful expressions of dissent. Their actions have been supported by the United Kingdom and the United States, which are both eager to see suspects kept off their territory and willing to turn a blind eye to arbitrary detentions and physical torture. Open Society's mandate includes forcing the agents of those countries to respect their own laws, even when they believe the easiest path to a conviction would be to ignore them.

The Justice Initiative has status with the United Nations Economic and Social Council and with the Council of Europe, which gives Goldston the right to lodge complaints with both.

He forced the European Court of Human Rights to hear Khalid El-Masri's case while shining a light on the US habit of "extraordinary renditions." In response to 9/11, Congress had passed the Patriot Act, authorizing a number of covert measures to apprehend suspects who may wish to harm America or its citizens abroad. Suspects can be picked up in any cooperating country and transported to other countries where torture is common practice in prisons. As a signatory to the UN Convention Against Torture and the Geneva Conventions that prohibit "outrages upon personal dignity," the US government had every reason to keep within the boundaries of international law, but 9/11 trumped such concerns. As President George W. Bush pointed out at the time, the need to protect American lives was greater than the niceties of prior decisions. The United States set up a system that could and would ignore the objections of human rights groups and use "enhanced interrogation techniques" when and where it deemed such methods were necessary.

Khalid El-Masri, a car salesman and a German citizen, was unfortunate enough to experience those "techniques" personally. On December 31, 2003, he was picked up by Macedonian agents in Skopje. He had been travelling on a German passport (his own), which the agents promptly confiscated. He was held in a hotel room for twenty-three days before he was handed over to the CIA. They flew him to Kabul where his interrogation continued for an additional four months. He was beaten, temporarily blinded, and denied the right to a doctor or a German government representative. He was finally dumped by the side of the road near the Albanian border at the end of May 2004.

In December 2012, the European Court ruled that El-Masri had been the victim of mistaken identity and torture by the CIA. Goldston, the lead lawyer for El-Masri, wrote in *The New York Times* that the court "held that the forcible disappearance and covert transfer without legal process to US custody violated the most basic guarantees of human decency." Goldston urged President Obama "to immediately and publicly acknowledge the wrong that was done to Mr. Masri, apologize on behalf of the American people and offer reasonable compensation to Mr. Masri."[5]

The United States did eventually admit that it had made a mistake, but US courts dismissed the El-Masri complaint on the grounds that "the very subject of the litigation is itself a state secret."

The European Court of Human rights unanimously found that Macedonia had violated El-Masri's human rights. El-Masri sued the government of Macedonia for transferring him into the custody of the CIA, knowing he would be tortured. Macedonia awarded him €60,000 in damages. Goldston acted as co-counsel before the European Court of Human Rights and Open Society's Justice Initiative helped Macedonian lawyer Filip Medarski litigate the case. Though it took a long time to come to a satisfactory conclusion, it succeeded in shining a light on the CIA's methods of torture and denial — a subject that has since been taken up by the media.

In 2013 the Justice Initiative published a damning document entitled *Globalizing Torture: CIA's Secret Detention and Extraordinary Rendition.* It records the CIA's current and recent practices, the names of detainees and torture victims, the status of their cases, and the countries that have colluded in their detention. Clearly, the CIA's definition of *humane* differs from most people's definition of the word. After the release of the US Senate report on the agency's methods, CIA Director John Brennan continued to defend what he referred to as "enhanced interrogation techniques" as useful tools in the agency's arsenal.

In a recent case presented by the Open Society Justice Initiative, the European Court of Human Rights has confirmed that the CIA operated a secret torture centre in Poland.

The November 2013 publication of Aryeh Neier and David Rothman's[6] *Ethics Abandoned* on the activities of medical professionals who enabled CIA operatives to torture suspected terrorists shone a light on practices that the United States condemns, but only until its security departments deem them necessary. No one was particularly surprised by these revelations. So-called "enhanced interrogation techniques," if the suspect was to survive interrogation, would require medical supervision or at least guidance, but abuses on this scale were beyond what had commonly been suspected.

The Justice Initiative has called on the European Court of Human Rights to look into both Poland's and Romania's involvement in the 2002–2003 detention and torture of Abd Al-Rahim Al-Nashiri and their role in transferring him to Guantánamo Bay. The pathetic performance of the United Nations Human Rights Council, and the ridiculous choice of its members, has made the European Court the best chance to force the United States to admit to its gross violations of human rights in the name of the "war on terror." It will not be an easy battle, but Goldston had also worked as a prosecutor in the office of the United States Attorney for the southern district of New York and knows the system well.

During our last meeting, Goldston talked of the many years of effort pushing the Cambodian government to effectively investigate and prosecute the four Khmer Rouge leaders it has arrested for crimes against humanity. The Khmer Rouge were responsible for the murder of about

1.7 million of their fellow citizens. During their rule, there was no access to courts or justice and no chance of avoiding starvation, torture, and death. Sadly, very few of the hundreds of Khmer Rouge who were involved in this brutal genocide will ever see their day in court. A young human rights worker, who spent weeks in the north of the country, told me that she had spoken with former high-ranking members of the Khmer Rouge, who are still proud of their rule and still supported by the locals.

The trials were finally set to begin thirty-two years after the Khmer Rouge were driven from power by Vietnamese troops in 1979. The United Nations–backed tribunal is officially known as the Extraordinary Courts in the Chambers of Cambodia. The most extraordinary thing about the courts has been their reluctance to conduct timely investigations to bring the perpetrators to justice. Only one person has been convicted so far: Kaing Khek Iev, also known as "Duch," who ran the Tuol Sleng torture centre. He has appealed his conviction. Three more ancient Khmer Rouge functionaries were nearing trial, but the government appeared hopeful that they would die before they faced being questioned.

Cambodia's prime minister, a former Khmer Rouge soldier, said in 1998 that it would be best "to dig a hole and bury the past." Goldston disagrees. "This is important for Cambodia, where so many victims have waited decades for justice," he says. "We can't look forward," he told me, "until we learn to look backward."

It was looking backward that led Goldston to bring the case of Sergei Magnitsky before the European Court on Human Rights. Magnitsky, a Russian lawyer for UK-based Capital Management, revealed to Russian authorities a $230 million tax fraud by officials at Russia's Ministry of the Interior. In 2008 he was arrested on trumped-up charges and died a year later in jail while awaiting trial. His mother sought help from the Justice Initiative to vindicate her son and prove that Russia had violated the European Convention on Human Rights.

Goldston said, "Sergei Magnitsky was wrongly detained and tortured because he unearthed evidence of grand theft at senior levels of the Russian government, then he refused to back down. Though Mr. Magnitsky's courage was unusual, his fate is not. His case shines a spotlight on the corruption and abuse which pervade Russia's justice system."

The application was filed by the Open Society Justice Initiative before the European Court of Human Rights on October 17, 2012. In November 2013 the court expressed regret over the lack of results of the "official investigation in Russia of Magnitsky's in-custody death and the impunity of those associated with it."

When I last spoke with him, Goldston had not given up. He is nothing if not dogged in his determination.

SIXTEEN

The Politics of Public Health

George Soros's parents died two very different deaths. Tivadar, George's childhood hero, the man who saved the family in wartime Hungary, died undignified, miserable, and alone after enduring an operation he didn't want. He was afraid he would lose his ability to think about death and that, in fact, is what happened. It may be revealing of Soros's nature that he let his father die alone, or it may be revealing of our society's inability or unwillingness to be near the dying. "I am afraid I kind of wrote him off," Soros said. "I was there when he died, yet I let him die alone. I could see him, but I wasn't at his bedside." Once Tivadar was in the hospital, he was no longer the father Soros had known.

"The day after he died I went into the office."[1] Soros's detachment from his natural emotions comes through in this statement, although he also explains that he had "kind of denied [that he was] dying."

His mother, determined to take control of her own death, joined the Hemlock Society, which promotes the idea of dying with dignity. Her desire to control how she was treated at the end of her life afforded the family an opportunity to discuss a subject that most people avoid. As a result, Soros said, her death was "a very positive experience for all of us because of the way she handled herself and the way the family … could participate in it."[2]

> Up to 80 percent of people die in hospitals, yet, for most people, hospitals are not a good place to die. They are set up to take care of acute illnesses, and dying is not an illness. It doesn't belong to an official medical category, it has no billing code that would permit reimbursement for the hospital and the physician. If you go to a hospital to die, the doctors have to find something wrong with you, something to treat, like pneumonia or dehydration, or they cannot admit you. They hook you up to tubes and machines and try to fix a condition that isn't fixable.[3]

It was his own personal experience that inspired Soros to fund the Project on Death in America. It was one of his two initial projects in the United States. The other was to spark a debate about changing drug laws. The Project on Death, like most of Open Society's projects, had a time limit. As Gara LaMarche said, "no matter what, the project was to last only ten years."[4]

The project began in 1994 under the leadership of Kathleen Foley,[5] a medical doctor and palliative cancer care specialist, intensely interested in the US neglect of the dying. She understood that society needed a fundamentally different view of the terminally ill, one that forced hospitals, nursing homes, and doctors to accept palliative care as a regular part of medical practice.

Her strategy included supporting the need for professional training among doctors, nurses, researchers, and educators so they could bring about change in turn. "What we all need in the face of death is compassion and support," Foley said.

"Physical pain is what people fear most about dying," Soros wrote in his "Reflections on Death in America." "In America, the land of the perpetually young, growing older is an embarrassment and dying is a failure." Soros, growing older himself, was keen to find a way to relieve the pain of dying. He was even willing to promote the idea of physician-assisted suicide. "I believe that people should be allowed to determine their own end," he wrote. The foundation gave $1 million to promote "dying with dignity" in Connecticut, but lawmakers defeated the bill. A new bill was introduced in June 2014.

Foley was guarded about how much was accomplished during the ten years of the project. She was reluctant to criticize the short duration of the Project on Death, but it was clear from what she said that ten years was not sufficient to change the way America treats the dying or to improve its ineffectual pain management regimen. Nor was the $45 million that Open Society spent — $5 million a year for nine years — enough to train and influence doctors. Still, Foley is proud of focusing attention on the problem. "We needed to have Trojan horses in the health care system," in order to change attitudes from within, rather than attempting to force change from the outside. "Our emphasis was on creating role model physicians."[6]

Until Project on Death, palliative care was not a specialty in the United States, nor was it integrated into hospitals. Now, more than 500 US hospitals have palliative care units, and others have taken on the task of caring for the dying. Foley is glad that Open Society was not the only foundation involved in working to change the way Americans deal with the dying. She gives credit to the Robert Wood Johnson Foundation's work in educating the public and in building understanding of the needs for palliative care. Other organizations took over some of her initiatives. "A good part of working for a Soros-funded project," she says, "is that you don't need to take credit. You can leave it on the table for others to claim." When she said this, I was reminded of the exact same statement made by Herb Sturz.

The International Palliative Care Initiative drew on the experience gained in America and applied it in eastern Europe, Africa, and Asia. Foley believes that its partnerships with others, including the World Health Organization, have ensured that many of its initiatives will continue after Open Society moves on to a new challenge. "We have seen some modest demonstrations of extraordinary results." she said in her final report. The results may be modest, but the project has been an extraordinary step in the right direction.

Until 2008, only Oregon had laws that "aid in dying," but by 2014, five more states had adopted new laws supporting dying without pain.

Public support for assisted dying has grown, but the terminology differs from state to state. About 3,000 people a year contact Compassion and Choices, an advocacy group, for legal advice to reduce end-of-life suffering. According to an October 2014 CTV News poll, 84 percent of Canadians support assisted death.

Easing the Pain, a 2010 Open Society publication, highlights the work of a small number of grant recipients who have advanced the cause of palliative care and pain relief in countries as different and far apart as Mongolia, Uganda, Hungary, and Vietnam.

In 2013 Open Society Foundations' Public Health Program expenditures were $44,762,000, even though there are several other foundations involved in health and Soros has tended not to follow in others' paths. His interests have been consistently political and he found that there are a lot of politics in health care. It is in this light that I looked at Open Society's activities in areas, such as HIV prevention programs, where public health is a political issue.

In Russia, for example, Open Society worked with local activists, such as Humanitarian Action, to provide a $24 million grant for needle exchange programs. In St. Petersburg alone, according to Open Society, there are more than 60,000 injection drug users, and many of them are HIV positive. Yet the government of Vladimir Putin has refused to acknowledge that a problem exists. USAid was turfed out of the country after Putin's last re-election, and the Global Fund to Fight AIDS, Tuberculosis, and Malaria will leave the country after 2014. In Russia, AIDS is a political hot potato, although Russia is home to the world's fastest-growing HIV epidemic. If you are an injection drug user in Russia, you likely have HIV, Hepatitis C, and more often than not, tuberculosis. For many years, Open Society has been a leader in the fight against tuberculosis.

Although the Russian constitution grants the right to free access to health services in government facilities, it does not provide effective care to those who have these multiple infections. And it bans opioid substitution therapy, which is the gold standard for opiate addiction treatment.

In 2013 Open Society issued a report on "Rights-Based Advocacy for Trans Health." The report profiles projects from sixteen organizations in twelve countries, dealing with barriers to health care for transsexuals — a group that faces discrimination and violence in many countries. The report uses data gathered in transgender studies across Europe and Africa.

The Mental Health Initiative funds NGOs in eastern Europe and the former Soviet Union that work to change restrictive laws or provide training geared to giving people with mental disabilities the means to live in their communities.

Open Society has also supported marginalized populations, such as the Roma, in obtaining health care and essential medicines. It has weighed in against the nefarious practice of the forced sterilization of Roma women in eastern Europe, and women with disabilities in a wide range of other countries, as well as women with HIV in sub-Saharan Africa. A new report, *What Works for Women and Girls: Evidence of HIV/AIDS Interventions,* was published by the foundation's Public Health Program, and its website provides access to 2,000 scientific articles and reports from 100 countries.

For Open Society, health care, access to medication, and harm reduction for addicts are all considered to be human rights.

In South Africa Open Society has supported a women's legal centre staffed by former and current sex workers, who can give advice to prostitutes. As a criminalized group, sex workers have felt powerless to confront abuse by clients and the police and to seek remedies for illnesses, such as HIV and Hepatitis C. Open Society's recent reports include "License to Deceive? A Big Drug Company's Smokescreen on Hepatitis C," "Beyond the Hype: What Sofobuvir Means — and Doesn't — for Global Hepatitis C Treatment," "How Social Accountability Protects Health Rights," "Advancing Human Rights in Patient Care: Practitioner Guides," and "Pretrial Detention and Health."

Marine Buissonnière, in charge of health spending, came to the foundation from Doctors Without Borders, perhaps the single most effective group that shows up in places where the need is greatest. She had been head of its missions in Korea, Tokyo, Gaza, and the West Bank.

Battling Ebola is another, urgent public health crisis. The inadequacy of the international response to the virus, the fear it prompts, and the disorganization of health services in the countries most affected have brought Open Society into the battle. Unlike most foundations and certainly unlike governments and UN agencies, Soros's Foundations have always been able to act swiftly.

SEVENTEEN

The Challenges of Climate Change

George Soros believes that humanity is well on the way to destroying itself through greenhouse gas emissions and that the United States must provide leadership if the catastrophe is to be avoided. At the 2009 United Nations Climate Change Conference held in Copenhagen, Soros suggested that rich nations should subsidize developing nations by tapping into the International Monetary Fund's $283 billion drawing rights. More than $150 million of that money went to the fifteen biggest developed economies. The fifteen developed countries expressed zero enthusiasm for the recommendation.

Soros then announced a $1 billion investment in "clean energy" technology and granted $100 million to Tom Heller's Climate Policy Initiative. Before joining the Climate Policy Initiative, Heller had been a senior fellow at Stanford's Institute of International Studies and at Stanford Woods Institute for the Environment. As his website attests, he is an expert on international law and legal institutions. Recently, his research has focused on international climate control, global energy use, and establishing legal structures in developing countries.

Heller has published many articles on climate change, including one that was included in the Pew Center's *Beyond Kyoto: Advancing the International Effort Against Climate Change.*[1] Since his appointment, he has spoken at a veritable smorgasbord of conferences around the world, appeared on panels, and produced reports and books about climate change and renewable energy.

Since March 2010, Heller has also acted as the vice-chair of the governing board of the Global Green Growth Institute which has its headquarters in Seoul, South Korea. Its mission is to help pioneer a new model of economic growth in emerging countries.

By all accounts, he is genial, dedicated, and knowledgeable, although he has yet to make a dent in US public policy.

Legislation to cap US carbon emissions was defeated in Congress in 2009. However that did not prevent the Obama administration from imposing a cap on emissions from the energy projects of the Overseas Private Investment Corporation, a US federal agency that finances international development. Other institutions in the West that have decided to limit support for fossil fuel energy projects include the World Bank and the European Investment Bank.[2]

The problem, as Soros sees it, is primarily a political one. As even the World Bank agrees, there is no longer any doubt that the atmosphere is warming. What is in doubt is what we can do about it and whether leading politicians have the will to deal with the issue.

Europe's carbon trading system has done nothing to decelerate global warming, said Soros, because it is open to manipulation. "The system can be gamed," he said at the London School of Economics. "That's why financial types like me like it, because it offers financial opportunities." Instead, he preferred a greenhouse-gas tax.

The following year at a New York City conference on climate change, Soros said he would focus on two initiatives: protecting rain forests and reducing coal's carbon footprint.

In its 2012 report, the Climate Policy Initiative suggested that there had been some significant policy developments at the national level. It singled out China, the United States, Brazil, India, and the European Union for almost two-thirds of the world's greenhouse emissions. Even in these countries, however, there have been some achievements in reducing emissions and local governments have shown support for new clean or biotech industries.

In 2012 China's 1.4 billion people were responsible for more than 10 billion tons of carbon dioxide emissions, while the one billion people on the entire African continent emitted just one-tenth of that amount. Africa is keen to catch up with China in industrial growth and its population could double that of China by the middle of the century. How does that bode for global climate change?

In December 2012, Soros repeated his proposal that the rich nations use $100 billion to set up a special green fund to help the developing world build climate change initiatives.

Through several of his funds, Soros has invested in green companies, such as Biofuel Energy Corporation; JA Solar, a Chinese solar company; and Transphorm, a California start-up that aims to cut electricity waste.

During our 2012 meeting, Soros cited one of his recent failures: "I was working on a project to change policy on rain forests." By the time it was implemented in Indonesia, it had become obvious that the results would not be what he had imagined. But one of Soros's endearing qualities is that he is perfectly all right with failures. You don't make billions speculating in currency markets without learning how to lose. Nor do you consider losing as more than another philosophical downturn if you are a follower of Popper's ideas and a believer in reflexivity.

Heller's Climate Policy Initiative has, of course, had a huge growth spurt since the funding from Soros kicked in. They have produced several publications, opened offices in Berlin, Rio de Janeiro, and Venice. They have hired experts and analysts and continue on their professed course to "assess, diagnose, and support nations' efforts towards low carbon growth. CPI answers key questions that policy-makers face."

Is it too soon to ask what they have accomplished?

The Soros-is-the-devil commentators now include the climate change initiative in the reasons why Soros is dangerous for America. Former Massachusetts governor Mitt Romney referred to climate change efforts as yet another Soros agenda. It seems that Soros's interest and investment in climate change has made the subject unpalatable for all those who view Soros's activities with overt suspicion.

Soros and Facebook co-founder Chris Hughes were among the chief funders of Organizing for Action, formed by Obama's top aides. Its goals include abortion rights and gun control, but its focus has shifted to include support for the president's plan to tackle climate change. The plan claims it will reduce carbon pollution from power plants by 30 percent by 2030. The administration is taking aim at coal, a move that would likely result in thousands of lost jobs.[3]

In February 2014, *The Hill* reported that Soros and fellow billionaire and philanthropist Tom Steyer had been to the White House for a meeting with John Podesta, advisor to President Obama, and that the subject they discussed was climate change.

On September 24, 2014, United Nations Secretary-General Ban Ki-Moon hosted a climate summit in New York. One hundred and twenty government leaders made speeches, but they did not announce any concrete proposals to deal with the problems of climate change. Although the United Nations cannot enforce promises that governments have made, it can spotlight the leaders' achievements and failures. President Obama stated that the US Congress would not ratify an international climate treaty. This is a reflection of Congress's belief in American exceptionalism — that no international treaty can be brought forward by those who are not US citizens. A positive outcome of the UN summit: about 400,000 people took to the streets in New York to demand action from politicians.

One stellar accomplishment was the statement from China's Vice Premier Zhang Gaoli that China would publish a date when its greenhouse emissions would reach a peak. Honouring that promise, US President Barack Obama and China's President Xi Jinping issued a joint announcement on November 12, 2014, that established a target for China's greenhouse emissions to peak in 2030 and decline afterwards. The United States proposed to reduce its own greenhouse emissions by 26–28 percent of the 2005 level, by 2025.

Canada's Prime Minister Stephen Harper did not attend the meeting. The summit aimed at increasing the momentum for action before the 2015 meeting in Paris.

EIGHTEEN

Ending the War on Drugs

"The European Union may be his main preoccupation now," Louise Arbour told me in 2013, "but his last great battle is ending the war on drugs." Louise Arbour is president of the International Crisis Group, an NGO committed to "preventing and resolving deadly conflict." She is a former UN High Commissioner for Human Rights and Chief Prosecutor for the International Criminal Tribunal for the Former Yugoslavia. She has known Soros for several years and is convinced that he will succeed in helping to hold together the European Union and end the war on drugs.

Aryeh Neier agreed with Arbour. In his declining years, Soros has had to limit major involvements, but ending the war on drugs has remained a top priority. Neier observed, "Criminalization is a strategy that buys into the notion that if you lock up enough young black males, you will promote public safety."[1]

President Richard Nixon launched the US war on drugs more than forty years ago with the goal of creating a drug-free world. Since then, several succeeding American presidents have supported the initiative. Yet despite more than $1 trillion spent to fight the so-called war, illegal drugs are now used by an estimated 270 million people and organized crime profits from a trade with an estimated turnover of over $330 billion a year — the world's largest illegal commodity market.[2]

In the nineties, Soros already supported a campaign to decriminalize drugs. He credited his friendship with Beat poet Allen Ginsberg with having planted the idea in his mind. His column in *The Wall Street Journal* on October 26, 2010, proposed that regulating and taxing marijuana would save taxpayers billions of dollars in enforcement and incarceration. He referred to the approximately 750,000 arrests for possession of small amounts of marijuana in 2010 alone.

"It is a case where the remedy is worse than the disease,"[3] Soros said. While it may be impossible to eliminate illegal drug use, Soros believes it is possible to reduce the harm drugs cause, both to individuals and to societies.

Ending the war on drugs, Soros believes, is the only logical way to reduce the violence in Mexico and South America and to start weaning the US public off trading in illegal drugs. He has pumped more than $80 million into the effort, most through his Open Society Foundations. Peter B. Lewis,[4] a fellow billionaire and unabashed pot smoker, added approximately $40 million of his own funds to Open Society's efforts.

Open Society's website declares: "Prohibition-based policies have led to a rise in drug-related violence, prison overcrowding, and an increase in HIV epidemics. The Global Drug Policy Program supports organizations that put forward alternatives."

Open Society is a sponsor of the Global Commission on Drug Policy, an organization focused on the decriminalization of drugs. Open Society appears to be just one of the commission's list of partners, although in reality it also funds some of the other partners, such as the Drug Policy Alliance. Soros sits on the Global Commission's board. He has worked with the commission's chair, former Brazilian President Fernando Henrique Cardoso, whose institute is one of the partners. Cardoso, a member of the Latin American Commission on Drugs and Democracy, has proposed extensive discussions on ending the war on drugs.

One of the commission's recent reports, entitled "Failed War on Drugs: A Federal Legislative Guide," cites four decades of government-funded, peer-reviewed medical research that proves the effectiveness of replacement therapies. The report proposes making these therapies available to serial hard-drug users. The commission also promotes replacing zero tolerance in schools with drug education for young people — the segment of society most likely to start experimenting with drugs — in the belief that drug education will prevent unnecessary deaths and criminal records.

According to the Drug Policy Alliance, the United States spends about $51 billion a year on the war on drugs. In 2012 alone close to 700,000 people were arrested for marijuana possession. The American Civil Liberties Union, another Open Society–supported organization, funds eliminating penalties for low-level possession and marijuana legalizing efforts.

At Davos in 2013, Soros shared a podium with Guatemalan President Otto Pérez Molina, who announced his support for ending the war on drugs. There are new ways of dealing with the problem now, claimed Molina. He told the press that drug money in his country has penetrated law enforcement and the justice system.

About one thousand people a month die in drug violence in Mexico. In some parts of the country law enforcement has given up on attempting to police towns; no one will run for local elections; and the army, when called in to deal with a horrific "incident," has no interest in finding the killers. Everyone knows who they are. After fifty years of the current enforcement-led, international drug control system, the war on drugs is coming under unparalleled scrutiny.

By late 2013, it looked as if the pressure on the US government was starting to work. Attorney General Eric Holder said that "too many Americans go to too many prisons for far too long." In an August speech in San Francisco, he questioned the effectiveness of the "war on drugs" and announced efforts at both the state and federal levels to reduce lengthy sentences for non-violent offenders. It was a speech that could have been drafted by Neier or Soros.

The use of "medical marijuana" has been approved in twenty-three states and the District of Columbia. However, even this limited use has remained illegal under federal laws, despite the evidence that it can relieve pain and alleviate the suffering of patients with cancer and AIDS.

No doubt, more research is needed, but given that marijuana is still illegal, research in the US is also illegal.

At the Summit of the Americas, South American presidents criticized the current approach to dealing with illegal drug use, and Brazil proposed decriminalizing marijuana use. The Organization of American States issued its Report on the Drug Problem in the Americas on May 17, 2013. This group is not known for radical policies or innovative approaches to solving old problems. Yet, this time, it succeeded in being both radical and innovative. "Criminal activity associated with the production, but mainly with the trafficking of drugs to the end-use countries and markets, is overwhelmingly greater and more alarming than that associated with retail and consumption," the report stated. "Facing the drug problem requires a multi-pronged approach, with great flexibility, and understanding of different realities." It went on to suggest that each country explore different policy options.[5] The report was endorsed by the governments of thirty-five countries.

Socialist President José Mujica of Uruguay pushed through new laws legalizing marijuana, despite opposition by the majority of Uruguayans. He insisted it was a way to neutralize drug traffickers. The new rules allow home growing, purchases of up to forty grams a month, and commercial production for medical and industrial purposes. Mujica would have preferred even broader measures, but he had to content himself with this modest beginning. Other countries will be watching the results.

Marijuana has already been decriminalized in Germany, Portugal, Belgium, Italy and the Netherlands. Canada may be heading in the same direction. Yet the Canadian government introduced mandatory minimum sentences for drug offences, while 2013 polls indicate that almost 70 percent of Canadians believe that the war on drugs has been a failure and 57 percent were in favour of legalizing pot.

Three US state governments, including Washington and Colorado, have finally passed new laws that allow small amounts of marijuana for personal use. President Obama's new "drug czar," Michael Botticelli, has been talking about "health-based approaches to drugs," rather than criminal prosecutions.

Speaking at an Open Society event, former Seattle police chief Jim

Pugel advocated treatment, instead of jail time, for low-level, non-violent drug offences.

The cost of worldwide drug enforcement is higher than $100 billion annually. At a time of global economic crisis and hardship for many countries, a hard look at the economics of drug enforcement, as well as its utter failure, is probably a smart approach.

Taking Control, published in 2014 by the Global Commission on Drug Policy, calls on all nations to remember the mandate of the United Nations "to ensure human rights and development." It points to the "overwhelming evidence" that proves the failure of the war on drugs and its "horrific consequences of punitive and prohibitionist laws and policies." The commission calls for "an end to the criminalization and incarceration of users, together with targeted prevention, harm reduction and treatment strategies."[6]

In 2016 the UN General Assembly will debate policies for the control of illegal drugs.

NINETEEN

The Battle for the Soul of Europe

As his great friend and admirer, author and journalist Kati Marton[1] told me, Soros has such a low opinion of human nature that he is rarely surprised by what we do to ourselves. Nevertheless, the near combustion of the European Union seems to have shocked him into feverish action — speeches, conferences, pleading in *The New York Review of Books, Der Spiegel,* and *The Financial Times,* as well as in his own books *Financial Turmoil in the United States and Europe* and *The Tragedy of the European Union: Disintegration or Revival.* He seemed to feel that time was running out both for "the fantastic object,"[2] as he had once billed the European Union and for his own life.

He brought together groups of economists who were encouraged to come up with new ideas for saving the union, funded new initiatives, and missed few opportunities when he could talk to politicians directly. Despite his avowed dislike for "talkfests," he attended those that had influential guests. He spoke at the European Union's Roma Summit (April 2014), the Global Economic Symposium (October 2013), at Goethe University's Centre for Financial Studies (April 2013), and at the Festival of Economics (June 2012), to name just a few.

By the end of the first decade of the twenty-first century, European banks held €1 trillion in Spanish debt; the Greek default on massive borrowing was an expected next step; Portugal and Ireland were not far behind; and, if you examined the balance sheets of Italy and France, you had to conclude they had also borrowed beyond their ability to repay. Vast numbers of young people were jobless and hopeless. The scenes on the streets of Madrid, Rome, Athens, and even Dublin had turned ugly, with protesters blaming their governments and the Germans for the demands for austerity.

Whatever new jobs were created were temporary and offered risible wages. The Mediterranean countries suffered from an inability to regain export markets, while Germany thrived on its own exports, much of it to the embattled Eurozone. The extraordinary profits of Germany's Central Bank were mirrored by the deficits of the banks in the loser countries.

Germans remained optimistic about their future. Their jobless rate had declined to 5 percent (it was 25 percent in Spain), their trade surplus rose, and their fondness for Angela Merkel's policies was reflected in the results of the 2013 election.

"Measures that could have worked if they had been adopted earlier," Soros wrote at the end 2011[3] were now too little, too late. This was the key to understanding the euro crisis. The much-ballyhooed European Financial Stability Facility was a perfect example of what might have worked had it been agreed to by twenty-seven countries a decade sooner, but it could no longer solve the problems of all the debtor nations.

At the 2012 World Economic Forum at Davos, the annual gathering of economists, statesmen, celebrities, academics, journalists, philosophers, and assorted pundits and windbags devoted themselves in large part to the potential collapse of the European idea — both the monetary as well as the political entity. Soros was there to warn of the crisis of global capitalism, coincidentally — the title of his 1999 book[4] — and to talk about *Financial Turmoil in Europe and the United States,* his 2012 book that stepped up the warnings. In the preceding year, he had turned his full attention to the declining fortunes of the euro and to the inherent problems of the European Union.

"The situation is eerily reminiscent of the 1930s," Soros wrote in *The New York Review of Books,* and blamed the 1992 Maastricht Treaty for failing to establish a real political union at the same time as it set up a monetary union. The Maastricht Treaty agreed to a common currency that lacked the backing of taxable citizens. It posited that the guarantees provided by a European Central Bank would be sufficient to lend stability to the new currency. They weren't.

Back in 2008, Soros had advocated substituting sovereign debt that was backed by the state for the credit of financial institutions where the viability of the financial institutions was no longer acceptable to counter parties.[5] This idea, of course, presupposes that the state has sufficient funds to back its sovereign credit. As the US government helped prop up its financial system after the failure of Lehman Brothers, the European Union could have used its collective power to guarantee support for its financial system. That did not happen or at least not in a way that would have had a lasting effect. Short-term funds did not remove the underlying causes of the crisis.

As Europe staggered towards the end of the first decade of the new century and into the second, it became obvious that the only country with sufficient financial credibility was Germany. The unhindered borrowing of member countries at what were, in effect, German interest rates allowed them to pig out on credit, and now they were threatening the viability of the union itself.

"The euro is a patently flawed construct," Soros announced with his usual tone of certainty, thus driving the euro even lower than its already precarious perch against the dollar. "The euro design does not allow for error," he said, observing that the Maastricht Treaty did not provide either an adjustment mechanism or an exit strategy, if a country could not fulfill its obligations. When the individual nations signed on to the common currency, they had "surrendered to the European Central Bank their right to create fiat money ... They now found themselves in the position of a third world country that had become heavily indebted in a currency it did not control."[6] A country with its own currency and monetary policy can respond to a decline by, for example, lowering interest rates. But the European Central Bank must respond to the overall situation of all the EU countries.

In his opinion, Germany, as the strongest and most credit-worthy of the group, would have to bear most of the responsibility for fixing the union and the euro. Imposing severe austerity on countries that failed to meet their financial obligations, he argued, was not going to work.

As he exhorted Angela Merkel[7] to risk disappointing German voters and belly up to the union bar, several formerly cheerful European Union member countries broke out in furious demonstrations of xenophobia. Even countries that had not yet felt the whip of serious austerity, such as Holland, were now openly questioning the benefits of belonging to a group that did not protect its members. France, usually allied with Germany on fiscal issues, was now unable to meet its own commitments under the European Union's Fiscal Compact. Portugal needed a new rescue program, and even tiny Slovenia was in trouble.

Soros's solution, as proposed in his January 2012 essay for *The New York Review of Books*, was a "two-phase manouvre: strict fiscal discipline and structural reforms of the deficit countries followed by stimulus. Otherwise, he predicted "a vicious circle in which economic decline and political disintegration mutually reinforce each other."

By then it was obvious that austerity was not working nor, given the massive debt burdens, would Europeans be able to spend their way out of the crisis. Yet, no new reforms designed for future growth were in evidence.

The European Union appointed the curiously named Troika — made up of the European Monetary Fund, the European Central Bank, and the European Commission — to supervise Greece's austerity program, expecting more taxes and the firing of more civil sector employees, teachers, police, and hospital staff, with concurrent protests and all-around misery.

Soros proposed a number of alternative measures to solve the immediate problems, but all of them relied on Germany. If Germany was determined to promote its self-interest above that of Europe, it would learn humility at its own cost, Soros predicted. "Germans are unaware," he warned, "that their prosperity was based on the debt the rest of Europe had accumulated." At that time, Soros believed that there was still a chance to convince Germany to show leadership and preserve the European Union. "The future of Europe depends on it." His plan was for

Germany to agree to loans at a concessionary rate of interest. The idea had been strongly supported by Joseph Stiglitz, at the 2010 Institute of New Economic Thinking conference in Cambridge. Stiglitz is a former head of the World Bank and the winner of the 2001 Nobel Prize in Economics.

"If the facts don't fit the theory, change the theory," suggested Stiglitz. "Austerity has failed. But its defenders are willing to claim victory on the basis of the weakest possible evidence: the economy is no longer collapsing ... But if that is the benchmark, we could say that jumping off a cliff is the best way to get down from the mountain."[8] In late 2014, he added that European austerity plans were a suicide pact. Germany was forcing other European countries to weaken their own economies.[9]

Germany did not seem to be in a mood to listen. Nor was it willing to take the blame for its own success — absorbing the cost of reunification, holding down wages, and finding a way to compete with the United States, China, and Korea, while its feckless neighbours ran up government debt and increased wages while their productivity fell. Not even Fiat could afford to stay in Italy. Germany would not bail out its EU mates.

Germany was even less likely to listen when Soros decided that an attractive alternative to Germany's leading the European Union to a new state of mutual support was for it to leave the union altogether, thus allowing it to devalue the euro, keep its citizens happy with less restrictive fiscal policies, and figure out a new way to live with its neighbours. "Lead or leave: this is a legitimate decision for Germany to make," he said in an interview with the *Financial Times*. "Either throw in your fate with the rest of Europe, take the risk of sinking or swimming together, or leave the euro, because if you have left, the problems of the eurozone would get better."[10]

Angela Merkel was not interested.

In an interview with *Der Spiegel*, Soros spoke of "a tragic, historical mistake by the Germans." He warned that Germany was on the way to becoming a "hated, imperial power."[11] A Pew research poll in May 2013, showed that other Europeans considered Germany to be the most arrogant country in the union.

If the euro broke up, it would damage Germany as much as other European countries, if not more. He attacked Merkel's elections bluster that Germany was strong enough to leave the eurozone and make it on its own. Merkel was re-elected on a platform that promised Germany could maintain the status quo. It could not.

Soros went on to propose that the "European Fiscal Authority, in partnership with the European Central Bank (ECB), can do what the ECB cannot do on its own. It could establish a Debt Reduction Fund, similar to that proposed by the Council of Economic Advisers and endorsed by the Social Democrats and the Greens. In return for Italy and Spain undertaking specified structural reforms, the Fund would acquire and hold a significant portion of their outstanding stock of debt."[12]

At the base of Soros's current perspective on the state of the union was his conviction that since the crash of 2008, "There has been widespread recognition both among economists and the general public that economic theory has failed. But there is no consensus on the causes and the extent of that failure."[13] Public intellectual Francis Fukuyama, author of *The End of History* and *The Last Man*, agreed that serious "debate is urgently needed, since the current form of globalized capitalism is eroding the middle-class social base on which liberal democracy rests."[14]

Seeking new answers, Soros funded the Institute for New Economic Thinking (co-sponsored with Jim Balsillie of BlackBerry fame).[15] It began in 2009 at Soros's home in Southampton, with a gathering of economists discussing how to change economics to open it up to new ideas. The conference included some of the leading lights of the profession, Anatole Kaletsky, economist and contributor to the *Financial Times*, Reuters, and the BBC; Perry Mehrling, former professor at MIT, now economics professor at Barnard; Ian Goldin of the Oxford Martin School; as well as Joseph Stiglitz, John Kay, and Jeffrey Sachs. As one of them pointed out, the gathering was "seriously financed," with everybody believing they could use their skills to "make the world a bit better" at someone else's expense. Stiglitz stated that, as Soros has maintained, there had been catastrophic failures in macroeconomics, finance, and regulatory policies. The situation was now urgent.

It is a subject Stiglitz has talked and written about for a couple of decades. His famous critique of the IMF's[16] "curious blend of ideology and bad economics"[17] — its outmoded standards that always bend to special interests — fell on deaf ears. The new model, Stiglitz said, was "open society," a way to try to influence standard thinking.

The group warned that Europe was "stumbling toward a catastrophe" and proposed that a "redemption fund" and a "banking union" were needed to save the euro and the increasingly fragile union. Time was running out, as Europe lurched from crisis to crisis with proposed measures that were inadequate, too late, or politically unpalatable.

Two years later, the institute attracted more than two hundred economists and policy wonks to its annual meeting at Bretton Woods, New Hampshire. There was a broad range of topics, but no resolution that could have shed light on how to solve the world's economic malaise. A common theme — that financial deregulation had gone too far and that markets, left to their own devices, cannot and will not correct themselves or the economies that depend on them — led to a spirited discussion. It is interesting that some of the attacks on deregulation came from the very people who had foisted it on the world: former US Treasury Secretary Larry Summers and former British Chancellor of the Exchequer and Prime Minister Gordon Brown.

In July 2012, the institute issued its statement or call to arms (rhetorically speaking): "Breaking the Deadlock: A Path Out of the Crisis." Its optimistic summary statement promised that it was still possible "economically and practically to find a way out of the euro zone crisis." The strategy offered to fix the design of the current governance model and provide a "minimal fiscal backstop" that would solve the immediate problems and give time to produce a long-term survival plan. The statement was signed by most of the members, but not all. Oddly, it lacks the signature of "advisor" George Soros.

Soros's September 2012 piece in *The New York Review of Books* is worth reading in its entirety, but I will quote only this:

> Since all the accumulated debt is denominated in euros it makes all the difference who remains in charge of the euro.

If Germany left, the euro would depreciate. The debt burden would remain the same in nominal terms, but diminish in real terms. The debtor countries would regain their competitiveness because their exports would become cheaper and their imports more expensive. The value of their real estate would also appreciate in nominal terms, i.e., it would be worth more in depreciated euros.

The creditor countries, by contrast, would incur losses on their investments in the euro area and also on their accumulated claims within the euro clearing system. The extent of these losses would depend on the extent of the depreciation; therefore creditor countries would have an interest in keeping the depreciation within bounds.

The eventual outcome would fulfill John Maynard Keynes's dream of an international currency system in which both creditors and debtors share responsibility for maintaining stability.[18]

Sounds simple, doesn't it?

By the middle of 2013, Soros was advocating that one way to save the European Union might be to get rid of the euro. "The causes of the crisis cannot be properly understood without recognizing the euro's fatal flaw. The solution, he had concluded, was Eurobonds. "If countries that abide by the EU's new Fiscal Compact were allowed to convert their entire stock of government debt into Eurobonds, the positive impact would be little short of the miraculous. The danger of default would disappear, as would risk premiums. Banks' balance sheets would receive an immediate boost, as would the heavily indebted countries' budgets."

The problem is that such a solution would require Germany's cooperation and with the financial burdens the new Eurobonds would foist on Germans, they are not about to jump at the idea. Hans-Werner Sinn, a professor of economics at Munich University, was scathing in his remarks about Soros's solution to the crisis. "For starters, there is no legal basis for his demand ... Soros does not recognize the real nature of the Eurozone's problems. The ongoing financial crisis is merely a symptom of the monetary union's underlying malady: its southern members' loss of competitiveness."[19] These countries, he said, used the euro's cheap credit to merely finance wage increases. His solution was price reduction in the southern countries and acceptance of inflation by their northern counterparts.

Soros fought back, charging that Sinn had deliberately distorted his argument: "Whether Germany agrees to Eurobonds or leaves the euro, either choice would be infinitely preferable to the current state of affairs." The proposal would mean that all twenty-seven members of the European Union would assume responsibility for all the sovereign debt of individual countries. While that would resolve the immediate crisis, it would come with staggering costs for the northern countries — a cost that their governments would be unable to convince their electorates to assume.

"Germany will not accept Eurobonds," responded Sinn. He seemed to echo Angela Merkel, who said that Eurobonds will not come in her lifetime. Nor was he interested in the proposal that Germany abandon the euro. "If the euro breaks up … Germany alone would lose about 545 billion euros." For good measure, he predicted a recession in Germany and warned that Europe faced a "slow death" unless it was willing to reform itself.

As the European problem continued, the Institute for New Economic Thinking set up a council on the eurozone crisis with seventeen European economists who discussed, debated, and blogged through 2012 and 2013 without, by their own admission, coming up with a clear solution.

During an Italian interview Soros said he had set up the Open Society Initiative in Europe, because "the euro crisis has endangered the principles of open society in Europe." It is guided by an "independent board" with his old protégé Ivan Krastev as chair. Open Society's 2013 budget for the Europe Initiative was $13 million, while $4 million was devoted to fighting xenophobia and intolerance. One of Open Society Initiative for Europe's first ventures was Solidarity Now in Greece. "The original idea was to generate European solidarity for the plight of Greeks," Soros told *Spiegel's* Gregor Peter Schmitz. By the time they got the project off the ground, though, it was too late to make a difference.[20] The offices are in Barcelona.

Strangely, Krastev's own view of the European Union's disintegration is somewhat different from Soros's. He does not believe that economic considerations are enough to keep the union together. "The very foundations on which the union was built are eroding," he wrote in an essay for the *Journal of Democracy*.[21] Most of the member states have lost faith in the effectiveness of the EU institutions. He suggests that there is a deep dissatisfaction with democracy," as governments are unable to control the "vagaries of the global market." He goes on to picture what the future could hold for a Europe reduced, once more, to its member states. While it is not a pretty picture, it is not as dramatic as Soros had described.

Undaunted, Soros told me in February 2014 that he was simply delighted by the news that Cambridge economics professor Lord Adair Turner will now be giving his undivided attention to the debate on the global financial system and, of course, will be shedding new light on the future of Europe.

I was thinking of the comment in the *Daily Telegraph* in 1993 about Soros's "increasingly grandiloquent communications to the media," and the hope that "the world's willingness to hang on Mr. Soros's every utterance should not fool him into believing them himself." Judging by his cheerful acknowledgement of his own mistakes, he was prepared to be wrong even at the height of his weighty pronouncements.

It is also worth paying attention to Soros's words about Europe: "As an investor, I would be very pessimistic, especially about Europe. But as a believer in an open society, I have to put my faith in the people and leaders of Europe to show some reason."

Soros's Quantum Fund had one of its best years in 2013. It added more than $5 billion to the George Soros's wealth.

EPILOGUE

Like George Soros, I was born in Hungary. As a child, I experienced Communism, a system of total government control where human rights were not even a buzz word, fair trials were an anathema, and the press was ruled by the government. Both my mother and my grandfather spent time in jail — my mother for attempting to cross the border to the West, my grandfather, a former publisher, for being critical of the regime. "The walls have ears" — a popular saying in our home and the homes of my friends — meant that the state police watched and listened to all our conversations. My grandfather had not been cautious enough.

I admired the help that Soros gave central and eastern Europeans in their struggles to rid themselves of totalitarian regimes. Without it, many Russian scientists would not have survived the end of the Soviet Union. The Polish, Hungarian, Czech, and Slovak intelligentsia who had been involved in anti-regime protests remember Soros's aid at a time when no one else was doing anything. Soros was a one-man Marshall Plan for the beleaguered. I know, met, and talked with many of the recipients of his aid. His extraordinary resourcefulness and the relentlessness of his commitment have been praised by most of them, as has his lack of concern for receiving credit.

Soros has said that he set out to "make the world a better place."[1] Unlike most people with similarly lofty ambitions, he had both the means and the ideas to make a real difference. He could invest in trying to change governments, donate to NGOs with special missions to destabilize undemocratic states, and help create international courts to accuse and try those who had committed genocide. By the late eighties, he was attending high-level meetings with politicians of every stripe and publishing articles in prominent newspapers about his latest ideas on how to solve the world's problems. So, after spending more than $12 billion over thirty years to make the world a better place, what is Soros's legacy?

Despite his gargantuan efforts, "open society" or liberal democracy is in worldwide decline. According to Freedom House, for the eighth consecutive year there were more declines in democracy than there were gains.[2] The numbers and stories speak for themselves, but if you want to be discouraged, look at the statistics on the Freedom House website or read Joshua Kurlantzick's *Democracy in Retreat* or even *The Economist* on the decline of democracy. Peter Mair's *Ruling the Void: The Hollowing of Western Democracy* is a finely written exploration of the demise of the old party system that had formed the foundation for democracies. As Chris Hedges said in his *Death of the Liberal Class*, "corporations, which are despotic authoritarian enclaves ... have infected wider society with their values." In the United States and in other nominally democratic countries, such as Canada, democracy is no longer the chief driving force in society. Greed is. Yet the mission statement of Soros's foundations remains exuberantly optimistic: "The Open Society Foundations work to build vibrant and tolerant societies whose governments are accountable and open to the participation of all people." It's a remarkable objective, given the recent histories of the countries where they have spent so many millions.

And despite the monumental efforts of Aryeh Neier and others, there has also been an overall decline in human rights during the last decade. Autocratic regimes now surpass democracies around the world. China may be the best example, but Russia is equally discouraging because it demonstrates that democratic elections do not necessarily bring about open societies, a free press, or a respect for human rights. We now know that they can, just as easily, do the opposite.

The European Union, Soros's "shiny bauble" that had once attracted eastern Europeans to the Holy Grail of cheerful co-existence, is in disarray. The economies of many EU members are under water and the squabbling in some cases has reached pre–Second World War levels. Elections have often favoured right-wing parties with xenophobic tendencies and strong leadership.

While Soros's foundations have spawned a new cadre of Roma elite, the average Roma is no better off than he or she was a decade ago. Most are still stigmatized, starved, and living squalid, hopeless lives.

The Arab Spring, once hailed by Soros as a new hope for the future, has been drowning in the blood of civilians murdered by opposing factions. Elsewhere, Arab rulers and army chiefs have indulged in autocratic clampdowns, a return to mass imprisonments, torture, repression, the arrest of journalists, and the exportation of violence.

Africa is still a mess, despite Open Society's widespread funding. Resource theft by local officials goes on virtually uninterrupted despite Transparency International, as does the pillage of Africa's resources by international corporations.

The country where many of Soros's people first met, Bosnia, has sunk into economic misery and the old ethnic feuds are still dividing its people. It is ironic that both Croatia and Serbia — the erstwhile aggressors — are doing significantly better than Bosnia, the erstwhile victim.

The International Criminal Court, an undertaking Soros has supported both verbally and financially, has accomplished very little at a vast cost. The International Crisis Group has been no more capable of averting atrocities than the United Nations.

The United States' perception of itself as "exceptional" has not changed and President Obama has not closed Guantánamo's prison, though the CIA's methods of "extraordinary renditions" have been replaced by targeted drone strikes. At the end of 2014, the Republicans retook the Senate, delivering a body blow to Obama's policies and the Democrats.

Soros's philosophy is still not taken seriously. Nor could I discern the influences of his thinking on his philanthropic activism. In my long 2013 interview with Istvan Rev, he said, "Soros had wanted to change the logic of operations in some parts of the world, not as a humanitarian, but as a philosopher with a world view to impart."

Soros, now living his third life as a public intellectual (speculator and philanthropist were the first two), is hated by many people throughout Europe and the United States. While that may be the fate of all soothsayers, in his case it matters a great deal because those who could change the way the world functions are not listening to him. When I last met him, he admitted as much himself.

In *Soros on Soros*, he said, "I am increasingly depicted in eastern and to some extent in western Europe, as stereotype of a judeo-plutocratic Bolshevik Zionist world conspirator ... My original purpose in setting up the Open Society Foundation was to create a society where this kind of conspiracy theory could flourish ... Don't you see the irony?"

Having decided, against his initial plan to close the foundations when he dies, having overcome his fear that they would become mired in bureaucracy, Soros decided that they could survive him so long as their chief mission "is to support civil society in monitoring the performance of governments." The ability to move fast, to be "opportunistic" when it comes to helping people is a unique aspect of Soros's foundations. But can the Open Society Foundations sustain that agility once Soros is no longer at the helm? Many of those I interviewed thought it would be impossible without his personal involvement.

EVEN FOR LIBERALS, Soros's philanthropic activities have raised some serious problems over the years. One problem, as described by Josef Joffe, publisher-editor of *Die Zeit*,[3] is that as "a statesman," Soros has not been accountable to the public and he has not had to stand for election on his record.

Another problem is the inherent contradiction between Soros the billionaire and Soros the philanthropist. When he lectures his fellow billionaires about the evils of unbridled greed, the super-wealthy 1 percent versus the rest of us, he makes no secret of being in the 1 percent.

He has made his wealth as a hedge fund manager, a speculator, using some of the obscure and hard-to-understand financial instruments that he has criticized.

Even Slavoj Žižek, the Marxist philosopher, who should be an admirer of Soros's social and political giving, has criticized him for his ability to separate the good he does from the way he earned the money that allows him to do good. Although he has become better known for his philanthropy than his business practices, "the former amounts to only a fraction of the effect of the latter." Shorting currencies has an effect on the lives of ordinary people.

Soros's generosity has also had some unfortunate side effects: money often corrupts and large sums can lead to excessive corruption or, at the very least, excessive pandering. As one insider said, sometimes during the past years the foundations resembled a royal court with a king and his courtiers. Yet Gara LaMarche's admiration for Soros's foundations has survived his departure from the Soros fold. "It is an extraordinary place, driven by a single philosophy of encouraging activities that lead to an open society."

As Churchill said, "Success consists of going from failure to failure without loss of enthusiasm." If your goal is to make the world a better place, you are bound to have failures. The question is how many failures can a foundation sustain and still lay claim to making things better? Istvan Rev believes that Open Society has remained fluid and open to change when it encounters failure. Failing is never the problem; it is just part of the process. "We constantly reevaluate what we do, how new strategies have to be invented in place of those that didn't work."

It would be ironic if the Soros legacy — as viewed through the lens of the next century — is the Central European University in Budapest. Ironic, because the one thing that Soros has never wanted was an edifice, a building to house his ideas. But it is also fitting because CEU may yet turn out to be the incubator of future leaders and, with a bit of luck, they will lead to a better world.

ACKNOWLEDGEMENTS

First, I am most grateful for the time afforded me by George Soros and Michael Vachon.

This has been a difficult book to write because George Soros's Open Society Foundations span the globe, and it is impossible to write about all their endeavours. It was difficult to choose what to include and what to leave out. I am grateful that I was able to interview the senior staff at the Open Society Foundations. They were generous with their time and with the written materials that they sent me. In particular, I wish to thank Aryeh Neier, Laura Silber, Istvan Rev, Tawanda Mutasah, Abdul Tejan Cole, Bernard Rorke, Herb Sturz, Ekaterina Genieva, and Lenny Benardo for their stories. Leon Botstein was particularly generous with his time.

I am grateful to Gara LaMarche for his reading and commenting on the draft manuscript. Michael Ignatieff's critical notes were immensely valuable, as were comments by Barbara Berson and Philip Cercone. Kostek Gebert read some parts of the manuscript and made some corrections.

I am thankful to Olivia Ward for her detailed notes. She spent time in some of the war-torn places where George Soros and his foundations were located and are still active.

I am grateful for the research grant I received from the Aurea Foundation.

I appreciated assistance from Ela Kinowska, who interviewed Ekaterina Genieva for me and set up my Skype interview with Ms Genieva. I am also grateful for the time Louise Arbour, former Supreme Court of Canada justice and former UN High Commissioner for Human Rights, found to talk with me.

I thank Professor Ed Safarian for his comments on Soros's economic theories and Janos Kis for his comments on Soros's philosophy.

This book would not have been published without the tireless editorial questioning, assistance, and fact checking of Diane Young and Bob Chodos. Without their help, I would still be researching and writing about the most recent news from the Open Society Foundations and George Soros himself.

NOTES

INTRODUCTION
1   Joshua Muravchik, "The Mind of George Soros," *Commentary* (March 2004).
2   Andy Sarlos, *Fear, Greed, and the End of the Rainbow* (Key Porter Books, 1998).
3   "Open Society Foundations' Expenditures," accessed November 28, 2014, http://www.open
    societyfoundations.org/sites/default/files/2013-program-expenditures-20140508_0.pdf.
4   Chuck Sudetic, *The Philanthropy of George Soros*, Public Affairs, 2011.

ONE   *The Messiah of Wall Street*
1   George Soros, *The Alchemy of Finance* (Hoboken: John Wiley & Sons, 1987).
2   Ibid., 372.
3   Slater, Robert. *Soros: The Life, Ideas, and Impact of the World's Most Influential Investor*
    (McGraw-Hill, 2009).
4   Michael Kaufman, *Soros: The Life and Times of a Messianic Billionaire* (New York: Random
    House, 2002).
5   *New Statesman* (December 2002).
6   Chrystia Freeland, *Plutocrats* (New York: Penguin, 2013).
7   Financial Services report (February 9, 2014).
8   Chairman of the Council of State and the last Communist President of Poland.
9   Dissident hero and first democratically elected President of Czechoslovakia.
10 Second President of the Czech Republic.
11 Leon Botstein, in discussion with the author, October 2013.
12 George Soros, in interview with the author, 2014.
13 Soros, in interview with the author, 2014.
14 Mr. Soros will be appalled that I have included such irrelevant details, but many people have
    asked me about his apartment.

15 Bill Moyers, "ACT is out of business and was fined $775,000 by the FEC. I don't mean to pile it on here, but then they were accused of sort of potentially violating the law." *Bill Moyers Journal*, PBS, 2008.
16 $1 million to Priorities USA Action, the Super PAC that backed President Barack Obama's reelection.
17 Reuters, October 24, 2013.

TWO *The Difficulty of Being Jewish*
1 Michael Kaufman, *Soros: The Life and Times of a Messianic Billionaire* (New York: Random House, 2002).
2 Jewish Telegraphic Agency (JTA), September 13, 2010.
3 Joffe and Steinberg, "Bad Investment: The Philanthropy of George Soros and the Arab-Israeli Conflict," *NGO Monitor*, May 2013.
4 J Street's website, accessed November 28, 2014, http://jstreet.org/September 13, 2010.
5 Ibid.
6 *The New York Review of Books* (November 6, 2006).
7 Joffe and Steinberg, "Bad Investment."
8 Ibid.
9 *FrontPage Mag* (June 27, 2011).
10 George Soros, *Soros on Soros: Staying Ahead of the Curve* (Hoboken: John Wiley & Sons, 1995).

THREE *The Ideas That Fuel the Man and His Foundations*
1 Karl Popper, *Conjectures and Refutations: The Growth of Scientific Knowledge* (Oxford: Routledge and Kegan Paul, 1963).
2 Sebastian Mallaby, *More Money than God* (New York: Peguin, 2010).
3 Soros, *Alchemy*, 1987.
4 Ibid.
5 George Soros, *The Crisis of Global Capitalism* (New York: Public Affairs, 1998).
6 Soros, "General Theory of Reflexivity," *Financial Times* (October 26, 2009).
7 Ibid.
8 Susan Porter, in interview with the author, 2014.
9 Soros at the Festival of Economics, Trento, Italy.
10 George Soros, *New Paradigm for the Financial Markets: The Credit Crisis of 2008 and What it Means* (New York: Public Affairs, 2008).
11 Soros, *Open Society: Reforming Global Capitalism* (New York: Public Affairs, 2000).
12 *Forbes* and George Soros.com.

FOUR *Mr. Human Rights*
1 "Rights Watchdog, Lost in the Mideast," (October 19, 2009).
2 Roth, in interview with the author, Toronto 2012.
3 Jorge Valls, *Twenty Years and Forty Days* (New York: Americas Watch, 1986).
4 Neier, in interview with the author, 2012.
5 Neier, in interview with the author, 2013.
6 Neier, in interview with the author, 2013.
7 *The Lost American Frontline*, WGBH Education Foundation, 1997.

FIVE *The Hub in New York*
1 Washington Center for Responsible Politics.
2 "Open Society Foundations' Expenditures," accessed November 28, 2014, http://www.opensocietyfoundations.org/sites/default/files/2013-program-expenditures-20140508_0.pdf.

3   Alexander Joffe, *Bad Investment: The Philanthropy of George Soros and the Arab-Israeli Conflict* (*NGO Monitor*, 2013).
4   Detailed financial information is available on CEU's website.
5   Liz Lorant, in interview with the author, 2011.
6   The Human Rights Initiative's budget, which was $50,817,000 in 2014, is shown on the Open Society Foundations' website.
7   *The New York Times* (August 12, 2013).

SIX *The Legalist*
1   Chris Stone, in interview with the author, 2014.
2   Botstein, in interview with the author, 2013.

SEVEN *The Hungarian Experiment*
1   For Neier's definition, see Soros, *Open Society: Reforming Global Capitalism.*

EIGHT *Eastern Promises*
1   Founded in 1977, Charter 77 was an organization of intellectuals whose membership included Vaclav Havel and Jan Patocka.
2   Statni Bezpecnost, the State Protection Agency.
3   Allamvedelmi Hatosag, also the State Protection Agency.
4   The Helsinki Accords, signed by most European countries including the USSR and Poland, guaranteed among other undertakings, "Respect for human rights and fundamental freedoms, including freedom of thought, conscience, religion, or belief." The agreement was not binding and obviously the Communist countries had no intention of living up to what they had signed.
5   *Transitions Online* was initially funded by Soros's Open Society Institute.
6   Sachs, in interview with the author, 2009.
7   Mark McKinnon, *The Globe and Mail* (November 26, 2003).
8   Open Society Foundations, "Promotion of the Fair and Open Election of 2004."
9   Leonid Kuchma was president of Ukraine from 1994–2005.
10   Poroshenko is a Ukrainian billionaire, often referred to in Kiev as "the chocolate king."
11   Soros in interview with Gregor Peter Schmitz, *The New York Review of Books* (April 24, 2014).

NINE *The Failure in Russia*
1   "Transition to the Market," a report released by Stanislav Shatalin and his colleagues in 1990, posited a process that would take 500 days to transform the country's moribund financial planning to a market economy model.
2   Igor Smirnov, "What Boris Yeltsin and George Soros Agreed On," (*Izvestia* 5, January 13, 1993).
3   Michael Lewis, January 10, 1994.
4   Aryeh Neier, *The International Human Rights Movement* (Princeton: Princeton University Press, 2012).
5   Genieva, in interview with the author and her colleague, Ela Kinowska, 2012.
6   Masha Gessen, "The Wrath of Putin," *Vanity Fair* (April 2012).
7   *BBC News* (November 7, 2003).
8   Masha Gessen, *The Man Without a Face* (New York: Penguin, 2012).

TEN *Meddling in the Balkans*
1   Aryeh Neier, *War Crimes: Brutality, Genocide, Terror, and the Struggle for Justice* (Washington: Crown Books, 1998).
2   Koncz, in interview with the author, 2013.
3   Vejvoda, in interview with the author, 2011.

4   Sonia Licht is a recipient of France's Légion d'Honneur and is president of the Belgrade Fund for Political Excellence.
5   Diane F. Orentlicher, *That Someone Guilty Be Punished* (Open Society Justice, 2010).
6   David Scheffer, *All the Missing Souls: A Personal History of the War Crimes Tribunals.*
7   Karadžić in 2008; Mladić in 2011.
8   *Transitions Online* (May 24, 2013).
9   "Building an Open Society in the Western Balkans."

ELEVEN   *The Struggles of the Roma*

1   Soros, "My Message to Europe," accessed November 28, 2014, http://www.opensociety foundations.org/voices/my-message-europe-plight-roma-can-no-longer-be-ignored.
2   I've seen an example of workfare in a village close to Mohacs, Hungary.
3   Soros, "Education: A Way Forward," accessed November 28, 2014, http://www.opensociety foundations.org/voices/education-way-forward.
4   The Roma have typically found work in central and eastern Europe as musicians.
5   Romanian sociologist Nicolae Gheorghe was a Roma representative at the OSCE.
6   Szoke, in interview with the author, 2013.
7   Rorke, in interview with the author, 2012 and 2014.
8   Jovanovic, in interview with the author, 2012.
9   *Human Rights of Roma and Travellers in Europe* (Council of Europe, 2012).

TWELVE   *African Expeditions*

1   Sam Roberts, *A Kind of Genius: Herb Sturz and Society's Toughest Problems* (New York: Public Affairs, 2009).
2   Jan C. Bekker, *Nepotism, Corruption and Discrimination: A Predicament for Post-Apartheid South African Public Service.* Prime Minister Zuma and several of his ministers have also been accused of nepotism. Also see Amnesty International's report on South Africa (May 2010).
3   Mahmood Mamdani, "The Logic of Nuremberg," *London Review of Books* (November 7, 2013).
4   Three military coups took place between 1967 and 1968 alone.
5   Zoe Dugal, "Witness to Truth: The TRC for Sierra Leone" in *Rescuing a Fragile State* (Wilfrid Laurier University Press, 2009).
6   Ishmael Beah's *A Long Way Home: Memoirs of a Boy Soldier* is a harrowing read.
7   Gberie, in interview with the author, 2012.
8   Diamond and Mosbacher, "Petroleum to the People," *Foreign Affairs* (September/October 2013).
9   Soros, *Open Society,* 2000.
10 Gberie, in interview with the author, 2012.

THIRTEEN   *Myanmar: Another Test for Democracy*

1   Timothy Garton Ash, *The New York Review of Books* (May 25, 2000).
2   *The New York Times*, March 1, 2014.
3   Daniel Bases, "Myanmar Investment Message," *Reuters* (September 24, 2014).

FOURTEEN   *Tackling America*

1   LaMarche, in interview with the author, 2012.
2   The Criminal Justice Fund spent $16,749,000 in 2013.
3   Matthew Bishop and Michael Green, *Philanthrocapitalism: How the Rich Can Save the World* (New York: Bloomsbury Press, 2008). Bishop is US editor of *The Economist.*
4   Sam Roberts, *A Kind of Genius,* 2009.
5   Matt Bai, *The Democracy Alliance* (New York: Penguin, 2007).

6   *Huffington Post* (September 27, 2012).

7   Soros, *The Age of Fallibility*, 2006.

8   John Cassidy, "He Foresaw the End of an Era," *The New York Review of Books* (October 23, 2008).

9   Daniel Schulman, *Sons of Wichita: How the Koch Brothers Became America's Most Powerful Private Dynasty* (New York: Grand Central Publishing, 2014).

10   Super PACs are "independent expenditure only committees" that may not make contributions to candidates, campaigns, or parties, but may engage in unlimited political spending independently of the campaigns.

FIFTEEN   And Justice for All

1   Goldston, in interview with the author.

2   David Scheffer, *All the Missing Souls: A Personal History of War Crimes Tribunals* (Princeton: Princeton University Press, 2012).

3   George Jonas, in interview with the author, 2014.

4   Goldston, in interview with the author, 20121.

5   Goldston, "Rendition Condemned," *The New York Times* (December 13, 2012).

6   Rothman is president of The Center of Medicine as a Profession and a professor at Columbia.

SIXTEEN   The Politics of Public Health

1   Soros, "Reflections on Death in America." *Project on Death in America* (January 2001–December 2003).

2   Ibid.

3   Soros, "Reflections on Death in America" (a lecture in the Alexander Ming Fisher Lecture Series, Columbia Presbyterian Medical Center, November 30, 1994).

4   LaMarche, in interview with the author, 2012.

5   Foley, in interview with the author, 2013.

6   Foley, 2013.

SEVENTEEN   The Challenges of Climate Change

1   *Beyond Kyoto: Advancing the International Effort Against Climate Change* (Pew Center, 2003).

2   Roger Pielke and Daniel Sarewitz, "The Political Problem of Climate Change," *Financial Times*.

3   Leo Hohmann, *Front Page Politics US*.

EIGHTEEN   Ending the War on Drugs

1   Neier, in interview with the author, 2013.

2   United Nations Office on Drugs and Crime, accessed November 28, 2014, http://www.unodc.org.

3   Kelly Riddell, "George Soros' Real Crusade," accessed November 28, 2014 http://www.washingtontimes.com/news/2014/apr/2/billionaire-george-soros-turns-cash-into-legalized/?page=all.

4   Lewis was the chairman of Progressive Insurance Co. He died in 2014.

5   OAS report on *The Drug Problem in the Americas*. Presented in Bogota, Columbia on May 17, 2013.

6   The report is available online on the Global Commission on Drug Policy's website.

NINETEEN   The Battle for the Soul of Europe

1   Kati Marton is the author of, among other books, *Paris: A Love Story, Enemies of the People*, and *The Great Escape: Nine Jews who Fled Hitler and Changed the World*. Like Soros, she is Hungarian-American.

2   A phrase coined by psychoanalyst David Tuckett.

3   *The New York Review of Books* (December 13, 2011).
4   Soros, *The Crisis of Global Capitalism,* 1998.
5   Soros, "The Crisis and the Euro," *The New York Review of Books* (August 19, 2010).
6   George Soros at Trento, Italy, Festival of Economics.
7   In an Interview with Chrystia Freeland at CEU, he accused Angela Merkel of being the creator of the European crisis.
8   Project Syndicate, accessed November 28, 2014, http://www.project-syndicate.org/.
9   Project Syndicate, accessed September 26, 2014, http://www.project-syndicate.org/.
10 Soros, "Lead or Leave Euro," *Financial Times* (September 9, 2012).
11 *Spiegel Online* (June 26, 2012).
12 *Spiegel Online* (June 26, 2012).
14 Soros, June 2, 2012.
14 *Foreign Affairs* (January/February 2012).
15 The Institute is also discussed in Chapter 1
16 The International Monetary Fund and the World Bank were both created during the Bretton Woods Financial Conference, 1944, as part of the world's effort to avoid another Great Depression and to ease the way to European reconstruction.
17 *Globalization and Its Discontents* (New York: W.W. Norton & Company, 2002).
18 Soros, "The Tragedy of the European Union and How to Resolve It," *The New York Times Review of Books* (September 27, 2012).
19 Project Syndicate (April 23, 2013).
20 *The New York Review of Books* (April 24, 2014).
21 *Journal of Democracy* 23, no. 4.

EPILOGUE

1   Richard Heffner, *The Open Mind* (April 12, 1997).
2   "Freedom in the World," accessed November 28, 2014, https://freedomhouse.org/report/freedom-world/freedom-world-2014#.VHf.
3   Joffe, in interview with the author, 2012.

SELECTED BIBLIOGRAPHY

The sources cited are only a few of the more than 300 books and articles that I read as I did my research. Among the publications I consulted were reports from the Open Society Foundations, *Foreign Affairs Magazine* (2000–2014), *The Economist, The New York Review of Books* (Soros is a frequent contributor), *London Review of Books, Der Spiegel, Eurotopics, Transitions Online, European Voice,* and many others, both printed and online. I have followed the Soros blogs, both friendly and unfriendly, and read interviews with Soros and his senior staff, wherever they appeared.

Anders, Aslund and Michael McFaul, eds. *Revolution in Orange: The Origins of Ukraine's Democratic Breakthrough.* Washington: Carnegie Endowment for International Peace, 2006.

Bai, Matt. *The Argument: Billionaires, Bloggers and the Battle to Remake Democratic Politics.* New York: Penguin, 2007.

Beah, Ishmael. *A Long Way Gone: Memoirs of a Boy Soldier.* New York: Farrar, Straus and Giroux, 2007.

Freeland, Chrystia. *Plutocrats: The Rise of the New Global Super-Rich and the Fall of Everyone Else.* Toronto: Doubleday Canada, 2012.

Gessen, Masha. *The Man Without a Face: The Unlikely Rise of Vladimir Putin.* New York: Penguin, 2010.

Hedges, Chris. *Death of the Liberal Class.* Toronto: Vintage Canada, 2010.

Heisenberg, Werner. *Encounters with Einstein and Other Essays on People, Places and Particles.* Princeton: Princeton University Press, 1983.

Horowitz, David and Richard Poe. *The Shadow Party: How George Soros, Hillary Clinton, and Sixties Radicals Seized Control of the Democratic Party.* Nashville: Thomas Nelson, 2006.

Kaufman, Michael. *Soros: The Life and Times of a Messianic Billionaire.* New York: Random House, 2002.

Kohler, Scott. *The Preservation of Basic Science in the Former Soviet Union.* The International Science Foundation. 1992. https://cspcs.sanford.duke.edu/sites/default/files/descriptive/international_science_foundation.pdf.

Mair, Peter. *Ruling the Void: The Hollowing Out of the World*. London: Verso, 2013.

Mallaby, Sebastian. *More Money Than God: Hedge Funds and the Making of a New Elite*. New York: Penguin, 2010.

McFaul, Michael. "Ukraine Imports Democracy: External Influences on the Orange Revolution." *International Security* 32 (2007).

———, Nikolay Petrov, and Andrei Ryabov. *Between Dictatorship and Democracy: Russian Post-Communist Political Reform*. Washington: Carnegie Endowment for Peace, 2004.

Neier, Aryeh. *Taking Liberties: Four Decades in the Struggle for Human Rights*. Toronto: HarperCollins Canada/Public Affairs, 2003.

———. *Defending My Enemy: American Nazis, the Skokie Case, and the Risks of Freedom*. Boston: E.P. Dutton, 1979.

———. *The International Human Rights Movement: A History*. Princeton: Princeton University Press, 2012.

———. *War Crimes: Brutality, Genocide, Terror, and the Struggle for Justice*. Washington: Crown Books, 1998.

Nielsen, Waldemar. *Inside American Philanthropy: The Dramas of Donorship*. Norman: University of Oklahoma Press, 1996.

Open Society Justice Initiative. *Globalizing Torture: CIA Secret Detention and Extraordinary Rendition*. 2013. http://www.opensocietyfoundations.org/reports/globalizing-torture-cia-secret -detention-and-extraordinary-rendition.

Osiatynski, Viktor. *Rehab*. Iskry, 2007.

Popper, Karl. *Conjectures and Refutations: The Growth of Scientific Knowledge*. New York: Routledge, 2002.

———. *In Search of a Better World: Lectures and Essays From Thirty Years*. London: Routledge, 1995.

———. *Open Society and Its Enemies*. London: Routledge Classics, 2011.

Rieff, David. *Slaughterhouse: Bosnia and the Failure of the West*. New York, Simon & Schuster, 1995.

Roberts, Sam. *A Kind of Genius: Herb Sturz and Society's Toughest Problems*. New York: Public Affairs, 2009.

Scheffer, David. *All the Missing Souls: A Personal History of the War Crimes Tribunal*. Princeton: Princeton University Press, 2012.

Silber, Laura and Allan Little. *Yugoslavia: Death of a Nation*. TV Books, Inc. 1995.

Slater, Robert. *Soros: The Life, Ideas, and Impact of the World's Most Influential Investor*. McGraw-Hill, 2009.

Soros, George. *The Age of Fallibility: The Consequences of the War on Terror*. New York: Public Affairs, 2006.

———. *The Alchemy of Finance: Reading the Mind of the Market*. Hoboken: John Wiley & Sons, 1987.

———. *The Bubble of American Supremacy*. New York: Public Affairs, 2004.

———. *The Crisis of Global Capitalism: Open Society Endangered*. New York: Public Affairs, 1998.

———. *Financial Turmoil in Europe and the United States*. New York: Public Affairs, 2012.

———. *George Soros on Globalization*. New York: Public Affairs, 2002.

———. *New Paradigm for the Financial Market: The Credit Crisis of 2008 and What It Means*. (New York: Public Affairs, 2008).

———. *Open Society: Reforming Global Capitalism*. New York: Public Affairs, 2000.

———. *Opening the Soviet System*. London: Weidenfeld & Nicolson, 1990.

———. *Soros on Soros: Staying Ahead of the Curve*. Hoboken: John Wiley & Sons, 1995.

———. *The Soros Lectures at the Central European University*. New York: Public Affairs, 2010.

———. *Underwriting Democracy*. New York: Public Affairs, 2004. First published by Weidenfeld & Nicolson in England in 1990.

——— and Gregor Peter Schmitz. *The Tragedy of the European Union: Disintegration or Revival*. New York: Public Affairs, 2014.

Sudetic, Chuck. *The Philanthropy of George Soros: With an Essay and Comments by George Soros.* New York: Public Affairs, 2011.

Szanto, Andras, ed. *What Orwell Didn't Know: Propaganda and the New Face of American Politics.* New York: Public Affairs, 2007.

Wilson, Richard Ashby, ed. *Human Rights in the 'War on Terror.'* Cambridge: Cambridge University Press, 2005.

INDEX

See also Hemlock Society
Ebola, 71, 142, 179
economic man, 42
Egypt, 27, 32, 34–37, 61
El-Masri, Khalid, 170, 171
El Salvador, 52
ElBaradei, Mohamed, 37
Elcana, Yehuda, 88
Emma Lazarus Fund, 153
Esperanto, 21
Estemirova, Natalya, 112
Eurasia Program, 65
euro crisis, 105, 191, 192, 197, 198
Eurobonds, 25, 26, 197, 198
European Central Bank, 192, 193, 195
European Convention on Human Rights, 173
European Council on Foreign Relations, 97, 105
European Court of Human Rights, 113, 127, 165, 170–174
European Financial Stability Facility, 191
European Fiscal Authority, 195
European Investment Bank, 182
European Monetary Fund, 193
European Union (EU), 14, 24, 25, 91, 100, 182, 185, 190–199
    and austerity, 105, 191, 193, 194
    and rise of right-wing nationalism, 25
    and Roma, 73, 126–136, 190
        See also Decade of Roma Inclusion
    and Ukraine, 103, 104
    Charter of Fundamental Rights, 126
    Fiscal Compact, 193
    in disarray, 25, 60, 105, 106, 190–199
    membership, 100, 106, 122, 123, 124
    Mission to Bosnia-Herzegovina, 165
    See also Germany; Merkel, Angela
European Roma Rights Centre, 165
Equatorial Guinea, 142
Extractive Industries Transparency Initiative, 142
Extraordinary Courts in the Chambers of Cambodia, 173
extraordinary rendition, 170, 172, 202
    See also torture

fascism, 14, 34, 37, 88, 91
Ferreyr, Adriana, 20, 29
Festival of Economics, 190
Fidesz Party (Hungary), 88, 90, 91, 100, 128
financial crisis 2008, 24, 25, 42, 123, 128, 159, 160, 192, 195
Foley, Kathleen, 176
Forbes's lists, 20, 112, 141, 161
Ford Foundation, 10, 67, 87, 156
Fortune magazine, 23

Forward, The, 34
fossil fuels, 182
    See also coal
Foundation to Promote Open Society, 15
foundations, danger of becoming bureaucracies, 66, 81, 203
Fox News, 21, 34, 157, 158
Foxman, Abraham, 34
France, 127, 144, 191, 193
Freedom House, 60, 106, 201
Friedman, Milton, 160
Friends of Democracy, 65
Front National, 25
Fukuyama, Francis, 44, 195
fundamentals (market), 42

Gaddafi, Muammar, 61
Garda (Hungary), 127
Gates, Bill, 15, 23
Gberie, Lansana, 140, 144
Gebert, Konstanty (Kostek), 53, 96, 97
Geneva Conventions, 57, 170
Genieva, Ekaterina, 107, 113–115
Georgia, 10, 65, 67, 70, 99, 101, 102, 105
Georgian Dream Party, 101
Geremek, Bronislaw, 95
German Marshall Fund of the United States, 121
Germany, 21, 26, 37, 50
    and austerity, 105, 194
    and the EU, 25, 26, 191–195
    and exiting the EU, 25, 26, 194, 197, 198
    and marijuana, 188
    See also Merkel, Angela; European Union
Gessen, Masha, 115
Ghana, 143
Gingrich, Newt, 161
Ginsberg, Allen, 186
Giving Pledge, the, 15
Gligorov, Kiro, 125
Global Commission on Drug Policy, 186, 189
Global Drug Policy Program, 74, 186
Global Economic Symposium, 190
Global Fund to Fight AIDS, Tuberculosis, and Malaria, 178
Global Green Growth Institute, 182
Global Witness, 142, 145
Glucksmann, André, 44
gold, 30, 122, 139, 141, 143
Goldberg, J.J., 34
Goldin, Ian, 195
Goldston, James, 74, 165–174
Goncz, Arpad, 87
Gorbachev, Mikhail, 100, 107–109
Greece, 105, 125, 132, 191, 193, 198
greed, 143, 160, 201, 203